THE
POWER
OF
POSITIVE
EDUCATION

**How To Improve Education
By Understanding It
And Knowing How To Use It**

by

Will Clark

R&E Publishers

R&E Publishers
P.O. Box 2008, Saratoga, CA 95070
Tel: (408) 866-6303   Fax: (408) 866-0825

Book Cover and Illustrations by Kaye Quinn
Typesetting by elletro Productions

ISBN 1-56875-057-9

Library of Congress Cataloging-in-Publication Data
L.C.93-083492

Designed, typeset and totally manufactured in the United States of America.

PREFACE

Although this is a book on the subject of education, it's not designed as a classroom instruction guide, an education theory guide or a classroom disciplinary guide. In effect, this book is not designed to teach teachers how to teach and how to conduct activities within their classrooms.

Instead, the information in this book is designed to help create an understanding social, administrative and home environment that will help everyone improve the quality of education and make education more meaningful to students. This information allows teachers to become more effective in their classrooms, regardless of their evaluated level of competence or the classroom techniques that they choose to use. With greater understanding of the total education process, teachers may be allowed to have wider discretion and more personal choices in those decisions within their classrooms. Hopefully, they will have more power to choose to do what they do best, individually.

This information also helps parents understand their roles and responsibilities in the education process and guides them in specific tasks to fulfill those responsibilities. Parents are the cornerstones for the success of their children's education, therefore, they must understand that role.

Students also have an important and active role to play in the education process. This book guides them in understanding that role.

This book is divided into three distinct parts to achieve these goals. Part One discusses many negative social influences that obscure and even prevent a reasonable and fair evaluation of our education system. No one really knows, now, if the education system —within itself—is effective or ineffective. Opinions of that effectiveness are merely expressed based upon one's perception of the purpose of education related to his or her personal interest. This part addresses society, generally.

Part Two, Success Strategies For The Education Process, is designed for use within the education system and for those who make education policy. This part analyzes motivation strategies, reviews the importance of defining purposes for education and suggests changes in internal course curriculum.

Part Three, Student And Parent Responsibilities To Develop Successful Students, is addressed directly toward parents and students. It emphasizes that a student's success is primarily determined by one's home environment, which includes culture, history and support. This part covers success planning, understanding success obstacles, avoiding demotivation and developing effective study skills.

Although each part is aimed at a specific segment of society, each part is also mutually supportive. The reader will have a clearer understanding of an individual part by reading all three parts of the book.

ACKNOWLEDGMENTS

My deepest appreciation and thanks to my good friend John Patton for helping to make the completion of this book project possible. This project would not have been completed without his personal efforts and enthusiastic support.

Thanks also to Bob Reed, the publisher, for his personal assistance and cooperation in making this book not only a book, but also a project book that may be used with progressive education programs and projects to help improve the quality of education in America.

CONTENTS

INTRODUCTION

The concern for education, training and literacy continues to grow in our society. This growing concern, however, has not resulted in any tangible or measurable solutions to the problem of student education or to the problems of job skills, workplace training and general literacy.

Most contemporary studies and evaluations of the education system have provided no meaningful or significant information to form a basis to improve our education system. Most contemporary studies have been conceptualized and performed in accordance with preconceived notions—and even for political and other self-interest causes. For example, the perils of the education system is the basis for many political platforms. The perils and inadequacies of our education system are also the basis for increasing bureaucracies, larger budgets and higher taxes.

In reality, an unbiased and universal study has never been performed to discover what the education problems are and what can be done to improve the effectiveness and efficiency of the education system. The question of "how can we provide better educational opportunities for our children" simply has not been answered because it hasn't been seriously asked.

The purpose for this section is to introduce some of those questions that should be asked. Hopefully, in analyzing some of the obvious questions, some useful answers will also emerge. This section will introduce problems, perceptions, educational emphasis and educational effects upon success.

Problems of Students

As students, teenagers and adolescents they are facing problems now that have long left the memory of most adults. While most adults worry about financial problems, job difficulties and marital difficulties, they don't usually understand students' problems as significant. Adult problems are more serious to them.

Students' problems do exist. And, if they are the problems that cause most of their heartache, then they are serious problems. They cannot have adult problems because they aren't adults yet. They cannot have marital problems because they aren't married. Everyone, however, understands financial problems, although the emphasis and purpose might be different. Students' problems are serious, because they usually concern matters of acceptance and rejection which affect their pride, confidence and self-image.

As they are growing up, they have nothing that represents themselves other than themselves as they are. They have no long history to refer to. They don't own homes, cars or savings accounts. They don't even have serious jobs. All they have as their total reference points are themselves. That's why, as adolescents, they are so vulnerable to personal problems and hurts. They have no points of reference other than who they are and what they look like. The more prevalent this total reference point of "myself" is, the deeper and more damaging those hurts are.

These problems are real. They do exist. It's not wrong for them to feel anxiety over problems they face in their school years. Some of these problems include: the hurt to be chosen last, when "sides" are chosen to play ball; the fear of being too ugly, too tall, too skinny or too short; the fear of having to shower and dress in an open locker room; the tears when they have no friends; the ridicule when they appear stupid; the shame when a teacher embarrasses them in school; the embarrassment of having to dress differently; the embarrassment of going to a party without a date; the terror of someone refusing to dance with them at a party; and the common fear of making mistakes.

Problems Change with Perceptions

Most adults, in their struggle for economic survival, forget the importance of these problems, although they suffered through those same problems themselves. Their lack of understanding these problems is simply a case of changed perceptions caused by a more important matter of economics. Students will soon evolve into this perception themselves, and those old hurts and fears will gradually disappear, if they haven't been too deep, or too tragic. Most people really do survive through adolescence, and they usually evolve into good, healthy, normal and successful people.

To begin a success pattern, students must become aware that the problems and heartaches that they are having are normal problems and normal heartaches. Every generation has those similar problems, every generation survives, then every generation forgets. They should be confident that they will survive, their hurts will heal, and they will grow into beautiful persons that people will love.

Increasing Education Emphasis

Students, today, are certainly aware of the increasing education requirements and education demands upon our education systems. Teachers are being promised more money and benefits to teach students better, more mathematics and science classes have been added to increase technical understanding, and lower kindergarten classes have been added to give students a head start. Supposedly, all this increased education emphasis is to help prepare students to contribute to economic advancement in the future. While increased contributions toward education should be applauded, there are some serious questions concerning the purpose and goals of that emphasis.

- Is this emphasis to help students compete internationally?
- Is this emphasis to prepare students for jobs within, that don't exist?
- Is the emphasis simply political answers, because real answers to economic improvement haven't been found?

The political and egalitarian purposes and uses of the education system should not be quickly discounted. Several researchers have presented findings and opinions from research and analysis of a major educational research program. According to the authors of that analysis, the complete research document was never fully analyzed or publicized, due to the massive size, and due to the initial findings—that were contradictory to political and egalitarian rhetoric that had no factual basis. Some interesting conclusions from this research project include the following: [1]

- It's dangerous to make exclusive generalizations about the purposes of education.
- Because current research usually fails to reveal the ways in which education affects children, we may have to develop other modes of research.
- Education may function not to upgrade the labor supply, but as a way to regulate labor demand.
- It may be possible to realize higher returns by shifting the balance of investments away from education and toward work experience or on-the-job training.
- Variation in levels of school resources have little effect on variations in children's scores on standardized achievement tests.
- There is conflict between those who think education should concentrate on basic literacy and those who think education should be an economic base.
- No research has been done to conclude that a more educated person is more easily trainable for an actual job.

3

- The bulk of research indicates that schooling does relatively little of what it always claimed to do—foster the cognitive abilities of students and thus assure them a productive niche in the economy.
- Our schools have persisted in trying to serve political ends (egalitarian) and intellectual ones at the same time. The result has been failure on both fronts.
- Schools make no difference; families make the difference.

This referenced document gives no definite conclusions, for apparently, none have been found regarding the value and purpose of education; and the output gained from the amount of dollars input. Some interesting ideas were formulated, however, that affect the way society should view the education process. For example:

1. Most evidence indicated that increasing the amount of money for education does not result in a better or higher educated person. There are diminishing returns on expenditures, for there's an optimum point at which any extra amount of money that's spent into the education system produces less results. Money is not necessarily the answer to better education.

2. There's no clear consensus to define a better education, or the purpose and use of an education. An education is not essential for trainability for most jobs; however, those jobs are inaccessible without specific educational levels.

3. High schools are not designed to prepare a person for a job —only to provide a minimum level of academic and social literacy. Rhetorical emphasis on job preparation creates confusion and ambivalence.

4. Schools and the education system are only alternative sources of redistributing wealth. It serves the same function as other welfare and social expenditures—not because it prepares students equally for economic success—but because it provides a comfortable physical facility that children from all the social classes may equally enjoy while they are there.

5. Surprisingly, survey results indicated that school desegregation caused more harm to minority children. (This finding was the basic reason that this massive research project was never publicized —it was contradictory to the purpose for the research.)

Educational Effects on Personal Success

The purpose for this analysis is to offer information and encouragement to students and their parents to help them make decisions concerning school, grades and quality of education. According to this analysis, the family influence—principles, values, history, cultural background and social standing—has more influence on a student's success than does the difference between a grade of "A" or "B", or the school that one attends.

This is not to suggest that a student should not strive to achieve the highest goals. Striving for established goals is the foundation of the success process. A person who doesn't strive for realistic goals will never be successful. Goals must remain inherent in the nature of a success-oriented person.

A person is not required to make high grades, however, to become successful. If it's unrealistic and unreasonable for a student to achieve high grades, there should be no degrading stigma attached to that student. A "C" student who's performing as a "C" student must have the same opportunity to feel as successful as an "A" student performing as an "A" student. Isn't it better for a "C" student to graduate with a feeling of personal esteem and self-worth than to become defeated and drop out of school—and ultimately from the success process? In the real economic world, are there not more successful "C" people than there are "A" people?

What's the Real Education Status?

Students might be getting better educations than they or their parents think. Perhaps those educations aren't used because they are thought to be inferior. Recent events, particularly political and pseudo-intellectual rhetoric, have occurred to stress and politicize the education question. The plea for better education doesn't invite prudent questioning.

A rational politician or self-centered pseudo-intellectual would be at a disadvantage by ignoring the "great education dilemma" of society. It's politically and socially dangerous to argue for rationality of the education question. One who would argue against improving the education system (spending more money on education) would be disregarded as an uninspired and unpatriotic person. That person would be assumed to dislike his or her mother—and hate apple pie.

The survey, identified in the reference above, poses realistic questions regarding education. These questions must be considered to determine if the education system has remained the same, has worsened, has been politicized or has merely been evaluated by a new set of perspectives by those doing the evaluation. Before this may be determined, some questions must be considered. They include:

1. Basically, what's the purpose of education—at which level?

2. What are the desired results of education?
3. Who should be educated—to which level?
4. Who is responsible for education?
5. What is needed to improve education?
6. Can the results be measured—how?

Each of these questions will be analyzed, individually.

What is the purpose of education?

The social question hasn't been legitimately and universally answered regarding the valid purpose of an education for an individual. There are four proposed reasons:

1. To develop basic social literacy
2. To prepare a person for career opportunities
3. To redistribute national wealth
4. To control labor input

Traditional understanding suggests that an education is one of the two basic requirements for success. "Get a good education and work hard; and one will be successful." How often is this advice and admonition given by a parent or a teacher to a child? Is this valid guidance—or is this the guidance that's merely considered socially acceptable?

Is the child who cannot get a good education, high grades, doomed to the pits of failure because he or she could not get higher grades? Without those high grades—a good education—should a child attempt to work hard to become successful?

There should be no disagreement that one of the basic and fundamental purposes for an education must be basic social literacy. To function normally in society, one must be able to read, write, do simple arithmetic computations, speak without embarrassment, and to feel reasonably comfortable in mixed society. Students who don't drop out of school usually achieve these results by the time they graduate from high school. If they haven't achieved these results, research suggests that the fault lies in the family and cultural environment—not in the school environment.

Schooling plays little part in those social literacy failures. Are those persons doomed to failure due to their lack of social literacy skills? No. They are doomed to failure because society suggests they should fail and their culture reinforces that belief. In reality, school grades and higher social literacy have little to do with most of the normal jobs in society. Anyone can usually be trained easily at most jobs. Many "F" students are inherently capable of becoming "A" workers.

It's reasonably easy to argue, therefore, that an education doesn't specifically prepare one for career success.

Most jobs require only the basics that are necessary for normal social literacy. These basics include reading, writing and basic mathematics. All other subjects in school help to enhance one's life perspectives, but do only little toward direct career success. Most jobs or occupational environments have their own specialized criteria and procedures that must be learned by any new employee, regardless of the educational level. These procedures normally require only the lowest level of social literacy.

If education is to serve as a direct source of wealth distribution, as in a socialistic design, that's certainly achievable. All children in a classroom environment share the same benefits of that environment, equally. Although the brighter, more gifted, and more culturally nourished students will probably develop into higher success situations, as they would regardless; while they are inside the school physically, they share equally.

Students, as well as their parents, are well aware that lack of an education impairs one's opportunity for success. Is it the lack of the education, or the attitude pertaining to the lack of an education, that limits one's success potential? Many employers require a diploma as a prerequisite for a job that doesn't necessarily require the skills and knowledge necessary to earn a diploma. Is this not simply an arbitrary and exclusionary labor supply process rather than a credible evaluation process?

The education system has something to do with one's success. However, that relationship cannot be accurately defined until an understanding of the true purpose of education is made clear. Education, presently, is a scapegoat for many egalitarian and social impulses as well as special selfish interests.

What are the desired results of education?

This question is also vague and unanswered. The understood general assumption is that the result should be that all students will go to school, become educated to prepare for a life career, and then automatically evolve into a life career.

Although this is a noble ideal, it's certainly not realistic as criteria for an achievable goal. An unachievable goal is not a goal. Consequently, the question regarding the desired results from an education must be fully explored.

One part of the desired result definitely should be the preparation of students to enter into a life career. A broader, more universal view is also necessary to support clear and optimistic success models and paths for students who don't possess the intellectual capacity, attitude or patience to remain in this socially expected and required pattern. Tradition, emotions, apathy, and political and social rhetoric have precluded the establishment of these specific alternative results.

Who should be educated—at what level?

The present education system of learning is not only vague and frustrating, it's also demeaning and demotivational for as many as fifty percent of those students competing within that educational process. The process is graded and comparative, which means that many students are comparatively ranked at less than average.

This graded and ranking system presupposes for those below average students that they are destined for below average success possibilities. Nothing could be further from the truth, for one's intelligence level is only one of the factors of success—and not necessarily the most important factor.

A major question of the education dilemma is, should all children really be educated together as only one group? If the purpose of basic education is to prepare students for college (and the purpose is not clear) why should students who are incapable of successfully completing college level work be forced to compete with more academically oriented students?

If the purpose of an education is to prepare one for a successful career (and the purpose is not clear) why should academically oriented students be restricted in their ability and potential to excel by waiting for the less academically oriented, or less inspired, students to catch up—which they rarely do? In this absurdly vague environment it should not be surprising that students, parents and teachers remain frustrated.

These frustrations encourage failure.

Although these frustrations of the education process may be tolerated, reluctantly by most people, there are two negative aspects that must not continue to be tolerated if society expects success.

1. One is that the frustration and ambivalence of the education process encourages many students to drop out of school, as a result of despair.
2. The other is that the lower half of the academically compared students is taught failure instead of success.

Many students drop out of school because they see no relationship between school work and reality. Their perspectives may not be far removed from reality. Nevertheless, a high school diploma is usually essential to permit access to many jobs. Another stress that should not be over-emphasized in the education environment is that placed on achievement of high grades. Students are subtlety taught that average grades or low grades are indications of inability to be successful. Aspirations, in many cases, are destroyed due to the emphasis on comparative grades.

Who's responsible for education?

To further complicate the education dilemma is the fact that no one is clearly responsible for education. Shared responsibility is no responsibility—and doesn't permit accountability. The executive branch of government is becoming more active in concepts and requirements. State governments are attempting to become more involved with the education process, by attempting to spend more money into schools and education, although studies reveal that money is not necessarily the answer to the education dilemma. A logical base must be established before money is needlessly squandered. County and local school boards have little real discretion other than to comply with policies that serve no educational purpose, other than to accumulate statistics to satisfy social, legal and political bureaucratic biases.

Judges have even become social, intellectual, and education experts by establishing one-man executive rule over some school systems, for the purpose of ending segregation, to allow equal opportunity for black children. In reality these attempts actually do more harm to black children in those situations characterized by stress and threat.[1]

People who should have the most responsibility over children's educations are the ones who have the least control. This includes teachers, parents and even the older students. Teachers are becoming increasingly controlled by accountability for students' test scores —not for a student's esteem development toward personal success. Parents are ignored in the schooling process, until the schooling process seeks a source of blame for a student's failure. Parents' opinions regarding purposes of schooling, methods of instruction, or alternatives of grading are ignored in favor of educated elitism—that apparently has proven itself a failure—since there is now an education dilemma.

The question of who is responsible for education cannot be validly answered until the purpose of an education is established. This hasn't been done, and it appears that no interest is considered to do so.

SUMMARY

Many influences, sources and concepts must be considered to improve the real education opportunities of our children. Only a few of those ideas and possibilities have been identified and explored here. Enough of those questions have been presented, however, to reveal the total complexity of the education question.

Improving the quality of education is not a simple task. A major conclusion, however, is that the family and the culture of the student are the dominant influences that determine the quality of education that a student will receive.

Even the best families and the most beneficial cultures, however, don't provide total protection from many negative forces and influences that tend to weaken one's natural resolve to become educationally successful. Part One, the next section, exposes and explains these social actions and perceptions that attempt to discredit our education system. These are identified in the next three chapters: The Dilemma, Ambivalence and Distractors.

PART ONE

OBSTACLES
TO
EFFECTIVE
EDUCATION

CHAPTER ONE

THE EDUCATION DILEMMA

Some important questions continue to plague the public education system in our country. The simple existence and persistence of these questions imply that the education system of our country is ineffective, and, therefore, should be changed—or at the very minimum—ridiculed. These major questions include:

1. Is there a real education dilemma?
2. Are our schools declining in effectiveness?
3. Are teachers incapable of teaching effectively?
4. Are students not given adequate motivation to learn?
5. Are schools' curricula appropriate?
6. Is enough money allocated for education?
7. How can education be improved?

Increased emphasis on the subject of education, including massive and constant media coverage, has tended to create negative answers, automatically, to these questions that proclaim that nothing in our education system is working.

Without a full analysis and discussion, we are led to believe that our public education system is suddenly falling apart. It must be so, since politicians and intellectuals are telling us it's so. Could they be wrong? Could there be ulterior motives to their negative proclamations? Let's examine the seven questions identified above to gain a broader perspective of the education dilemma.

The overriding question, is there an education dilemma, must be analyzed before any of the other questions are relevant. Obviously, if there's no education dilemma and everything is working well, then there's no need to waste time trying to develop corrective actions. If there is an education dilemma, then rational answers must be found to correct those deficiencies—if they can be determined. At this point, however, let's not get too far ahead of ourselves—let's take only one question at a time. Trying to answer compound questions with simple answers might be the cause of our current dilemma.

The Education Dilemma

There is a serious dilemma that negatively affects the quality and the results of educational efforts. There are even two of these serious dilemmas that should be analyzed separately to understand their negative influences on education. The question regarding the education dilemma itself cannot be fairly answered until these two negative influences upon the education system are understood.

A Weakening Society

The first negative influence, a dilemma, is the weakening of our traditional social system. Our society is changing, rapidly, in ways that don't support traditional family compositions, which is the basic foundation that determines the quality of a student's learning. A significant point must be acknowledged to make this concept clear—the education dilemma is not related to the top sixty to seventy percent of those students who come from traditional middle-class families that support and reinforce educational efforts and learning skills. The education dilemma is created by the other thirty to forty percent who are born and reared in lower cultural environments that have no history or role models for success or educational aspirations. Without an inordinate amount of special attention to these deprived students, inside the classroom as well as outside the classroom, many of these students simply will not be successful. Their failure in the education system is only a part of the total failure package that they face. Their failure in the education process is not caused by the education process.

A reduced student-teacher ratio will most likely not significantly improve results for most of those deprived students. Teachers with reduced student-teacher ratios might tend to try harder to improve the education results of these weaker academic and less inspired students. If this were to occur, those more academically-oriented students—if in the same class—might not be allowed to develop their effective potential. This leaves, basically, only two reasonable alternatives. One alternative is to continue teaching in the traditional manner. The other alternative is to create special classes, with professional counselling, for those more culturally deprived students.

At this time, society doesn't support special separation of culturally deprived students. The fundamental assumption by sociologists and politicos is that those weaker students will be enriched by absorbing cultural and intellectual influences from students from middle class society who exhibit high aspirations and expectations. Consequently, our education system is forced to treat all students exactly alike. They are assumed to be, equally, blank spaces ready to be filled with education.

This is an unreasonable social assumption that places unreasonable and unfair demands upon the public education system.

Although many people, maybe most, understand the social and cultural influences that inhibit a child's ability to develop positive aspirations that will permit him or her to learn, and to take advantage of the education system, that problem is too great for society to address. It's easier and more convenient to blame the lack of education effectiveness for those thirty to forty percent of students on inefficiencies of the education system than on the real source. Educators should be accountable for teaching. They should not be accountable for a student's learning. That accountability should belong to the student—and at least equally to the parent.

This general social dilemma is created by the breakup of traditional family systems, by children having no positive role models in their families, by conflicting social and moral values and by unattended or unsupervised children. Two other special social conditions also apply. These include peer pressure to fail and lifestyle alternatives.

Peer pressure is a strong influence that determines the success or failure of many people. Peer pressure is especially strong in the lower cultures of society, for it's used as a tool to discourage someone who has potential and high aspirations from achieving those aspirations. Anyone who tries to be different in a culture that expects and accepts minimum success is often accused of trying to "be better than everybody else," or "snobbish." This pressure and intimidation creates a serious problem for anyone who wants to develop his or her potential. That person must make a conscious choice of whether to abandon his or her familiar friends and surroundings to be successful, or to remain in his or her perceived social and cultural position. One choice is a risk, and the other is stable security among friends.

Our society also permits expanded lifestyle alternatives that often discourage aspirations of success. Traditionally, a person had a choice of advancing one's education, beginning a job and a career or depending upon his or her family for sustained support. Since the mid 1960s another choice has been added to that list of alternatives. That choice is governmental support, primarily through the social welfare system. Those students who are only marginally motivated to succeed now have less reason to try to become personally success-ful, since they understand that the government will "take care of them."

These are social influences that aren't categorized by our society as social dilemmas. These are the negative influences that are interpreted by society as being the education dilemma since these influences create a negative atmosphere in the education system.

Educators aren't allowed to do what they have been charged to do in society—that is to teach. Instead, educators must defend themselves in the education arena, for they have been charged by society to correct society's problems. It's assumed by many in society that educators should motivate a child to want to learn, and to motivate a child to desire success. This task is impossible in most cases, for the most important influence on a child's aspirations is the child's home and cultural environments. An educator, except under unusual circumstances, cannot correct the damage that's done to a child in the child's nurturing and cultural environment. Many teachers have become frustrated and ambivalent, for they really try to accomplish this impossible task that's been forced onto them by society's acquiescence.

A Weakening Economic Leadership

The second negative influence, also a dilemma, is the economic weakness of our country. Economic weakness, or a declining economy, occurs in cycles throughout a nation's history. There are some good times and some bad times, economically.

A trend has occurred recently, however, that requires a new appraisal. This new trend suggests the possibility that our current weak economic condition is not caused by the normal ebb and flow of normal economic business cycles. Many actions suggest the real possibility that the strength, courage and stability of leadership in our country are weakening and disintegrating. This declining condition of leadership strength also points the finger toward education in an attempt to find a scapegoat to protect itself. Again, it's called the education dilemma, not the country's leadership dilemma.

Political, social and business leadership in America has been declining in effectiveness and in integrity for the past two decades. During the past two decades industrial and business leaders have failed to gain the respect and cooperation from their employees and other subordinates. This failure to offer hope and aspirations to those subordinates has resulted in a deep feeling of alienation by those subordinates. That alienation has grown to the degree that many workplaces operate under the concept of we and them, not under the concept of mutual interests and mutual goals.

At the same time of this growing alienation, American leaders began to question their leadership concepts and styles. During the early 1900s, autocratic leadership—the classical style—was the only known leadership style, since the study of leadership had just begun to be a serious consideration. This was caused by the industrial revolution, and the move away from craftsmanship and apprenticeships. Later, in the 1930s, human relations leadership, or democratic leadership, was discovered. These two concepts jockeyed for a dominant position in the workplace until the early 1970s.

Beginning in the 1970s, leaders could not understand the growing alienation and the lack of aggressive motivation by their workforces. They began to assume that their leadership styles were wrong, and that they should convert to a new leadership miracle— the Japanese leadership style. The Japanese leadership style, as interpreted by American leaders, was a shared leadership style that gave workers more control over their decisions in the workplace. To allow workers to have more freedom, American leadership began to eliminate many layers of middle and lower management and supervision. Basically, the new organization structure was to be senior leaders and first line workers. This is regarded as a flat organizational structure.

Senior leaders overlooked two important considerations in their attempt to save money by eliminating too many management layers, and by trying to motivate workers by giving them more decision-making authority. One of those considerations was the realization by those workers that they had no intermediate success ladders to advance themselves and to gain more recognition within their companies. They realized that they would probably be exploited workers for the rest of their career. Leaders assumed that merely increasing the pay of those workers for their more involved performance would continue to be a motivator. Motivational theories discount this assumption.

The second consideration, and probably the most important since it's related to the education dilemma, is that workers were expected to perform higher level tasks and to be more adept at decision-making to replace the supervisors and managers that had been removed from those intermediary levels. Many workers are not trained or emotionally prepared to assume those higher level decision tasks. Since many of those workers were not prepared to assume those higher level tasks that had been performed by supervisors and middle managers, higher leadership was forced to find a rational answer for their miscalculation. Their self-defensive rationalization is that the education system is not producing trained and qualified workers for business and industry.

The problem is that schools are not preparing students to begin a job with those higher skills that business leadership needs to eliminate that decision-making level and training level that's traditionally existed in business and industry. Schools get criticised by business leaders for not providing that level of worker, when in fact, traditional schools have never been tasked with that goal or that charter. Traditionally, the education system has been tasked with giving students only the basic information to make logical decisions for themselves within a societal structure. One of those alternatives that students may choose is to become trained in a skill or a trade.

That training must be done in the working environment, after a business selects a candidate who has demonstrated that he or she has a high probability of learning the job assignment. That training must be done in the job environment, not necessarily in the secondary education environment. Business and industrial leaders are more often ignoring this responsibility, and in the process are criticising the education system for their own weakness, inability or reluctance to provide that training.

Most complaints of the education system are generated by industrial and business leaders. That's more prudent for themselves than admitting that they have become frustrated and ambivalent with their primary purpose and charter, which should be to increase productivity by providing leadership that will inspire and motivate workers to be efficient and productive.

In the past several years this charter of leaders has been replaced with company financial manipulation to show quick short-term profits, and exploitation of workers also to show increased short-term profits. Business and industrial leadership, as well as political leadership, has lost its ability to provide inspiration, honesty, equity, motivation and long-term positive results.

Results of the Dilemma

Fundamental problems with our society and the defensive rhetoric of influential leaders in our country place critical pressure on our education system to perform beyond its current ability to perform. Our schools can provide only what they have been designed to provide, not what each special interest group decides schools should provide. Schools cannot form the basis for a new and equitable society to insure that each person achieves his or her highest level of potential. Schools provide only a part of that training. Home, culture and more basic nurturing environments have more influential force on those aspirations.

Schools cannot prepare workers for all jobs. Neither can schools assure students that they will be fairly, equitably and honestly treated when they enter into the workforce. Students often fail to become motivated toward jobs since the base of good jobs has rapidly declined. Why should they objectively and diligently prepare for good jobs when good jobs are becoming more scarce in this country? Schools have no influence over the quality of leadership in business and industry. Neither do they have the responsibility that business, industrial and political leaders do to insure that job conditions and leadership conditions are strong enough to offer motivation, anticipation and expectation for students when they become workers.

There is a social dilemma in our country, there is a leadership dilemma in our country and there is an economic dilemma in our country. It's unlikely that the existence of an education dilemma can be determined until these conditions are resolved. It's also improbable that the actual effectiveness of our education system may be determined until a clear purpose for our education system is defined. A clear purpose for our education system doesn't exist.

School Effectiveness

The next question is, "Are our schools declining in effectiveness?" The answer to this question remains partially camouflaged by the rhetoric initiated by the two conditions identified above. The rhetoric is so strong and vocal by social and business forces that the effectiveness of schools hasn't been objectively and fairly evaluated. Any evaluation or analysis is prequalified to produce a negative finding. An evaluator or a researcher who would produce a positive result of school effectiveness would be considered a social outcast, as well as a brainwashed incompetent.

Practically speaking, it's impossible to judge or to evaluate the effectiveness of our education system. A system, or an entity cannot be judged on its effectiveness if a clear purpose for its existence hasn't been established or conceptualized. This simply hasn't been done for our education system. The purpose or the goal of our education system is as varied as there are numbers of people who express an opinion. For example, the following ideas have been expressed as some purposes or goals of education:

1. To develop one's ability to find truth
2. To learn to find one's inner beauty
3. To develop an informed electorate
4. To develop social skills
5. To learn career skills
6. To develop equality of opportunity
7. To promote equality through socialization
8. To prepare a student for self-actualization

Even though this list shows only a few of the ideas of a purpose for education, it's complex enough to demonstrate that a valid evaluation of the effectiveness of education might be improbable. Therefore, only some basic fundamentals that may or may not indicate education effectiveness will be considered. These include numbers of students receiving diplomas, teacher qualifications and student scores and grades.

A larger percentage of the population is receiving high school diplomas today than ever before. In the early 1900s, most students were fortunate to earn a diploma at the eighth grade level. Only very few earned a diploma at the twelfth grade level. Many children were never counted in the education process, for they never entered into the school system, even at the first grade level. Today, approximately seventy percent of our children (the exact figure is unknown) completes the twelfth grade to earn a high school diploma. Of course, there's much controversy over the value of that high school diploma. However, that controversy is the basis of the alleged education dilemma.

Teacher qualifications and teacher accountability are topics that are frequently discussed, regarding the education dilemma. In years past, the success of a student was interpreted to result from the ability and the efforts of that student. Teachers were assumed to be in a classroom to teach various subjects. The growing trend, today, is that teachers should be graded and accountable for student grades on standardized achievement tests. The assumption by social and political evaluators is that the teacher should be measured—not the industriousness of the student.

In this intimidating and unrealistic education arena, the real value and effectiveness of teachers cannot be measured or evaluated in relation to the success of students. Teachers may be evaluated and judged on their ability to help students pass standardized tests; but, passing those standardized tests is not necessarily a measurement of a student's ability to succeed in a normally competitive society. Often, those things that teachers say, do and demonstrate that might not be directly related to grades and scores have more effect upon a child's eventual success than those more graded factors. The new trend toward specific, standardized and graded teacher accountability reduces the time that some teachers have to provide real success leadership and meaningful aspirations to many needy children, especially those who are culturally deprived.

Grades are not necessarily a determinant of social or economic success. A "C" student is as likely to be as socially and economically successful as an "A" student. Those success determinants are the levels of aspirations and expectations, family support, career choices and a magic spark that anyone may provide—even a teacher that might be evaluated as a weak teacher, according to modern evaluations.

Even those growing suggestions that students' grades are deteriorating have no basis in fact. Research and surveys show that grade disparities are usually within schools, not among schools. Schools considered weak, by ratio, have the same level of top students as do schools that are considered superior. Each school has high achievers, average achievers and low achievers. The quality of students in a school is, therefore, determined by the depth of students who are low achievers. This depth of low achievers is traditionally determined by the culture and social environment of those students. To repeat what has already been emphasized, schools that have a larger proportion of students from lower cultures, lower social groups and families that have lower aspirations will have a larger proportion of students who are not success oriented. Even these schools, however, will have some highly academically oriented and successful students.

Notwithstanding that a clear model for comparison doesn't exist (a clear purpose for education has not been established,) a valid claim that our education system is declining in effectiveness cannot be made. More students are receiving educations and diplomas today than ever before, the education level of most teachers is higher than ever before, and the same range of student grades, within schools, is no lower than historical averages. Internally, our schools are not declining in effectiveness. It's amazing that they continue to function at an effective level, with the increasing negative pressure from society that offers only negativism and intimidation—not real support.

Student Motivation

Another important question regarding education is that which concerns a student's motivation to learn. Many in our society are asking the question, "Why are our students not motivated to learn and to apply themselves in school to be successful?" A more appropriate question should be, "Why are we, as members of society, discouraging those students from finding a base upon which to develop their own natural motivation?" Motivation will be discussed more thoroughly in another chapter; however, it should be discussed briefly here to place motivation in proper perspective with the perceived education dilemma. Motivation is, after all, the driving force that determines the actions and reactions in any environment. Without motivation, nothing happens.

The question of student motivation may take two dimensions. One of those dimensions is the assumption that students, as well as everyone else, are empty shells waiting to be fed something called "motivation" to make them do something. This is the traditional view, outside the consideration of normal instincts, and the basis for most motivational theories. This interpretation is that a person responds to an outside stimulus to take action to fulfill a need.

Another dimension that's rarely considered is the idea that people are naturally and internally motivated to explore, to experiment and to develop themselves into a condition identified as self-actualization. This dimension assumes that people are naturally motivated and will continue to fulfill aspirations and advance themselves until and unless something happens to create a condition of demotivation. A condition of demotivation occurs rather than the absence of motivation. Motivation naturally exists, it's just suppressed by a psychological block of demotivation.

As an example of this concept, consider the normal development of a child. Most of these normal child tendencies were documented by Jean Piaget, a person often referenced in childhood learning and development. Piaget, born in 1896, received his doctorate in biological science at the age of twenty-five.[2]

In a child's normal development, that child goes through certain scheduled phases. Each of those phases involves trial, error and assimilation of physical movements with some result. For example, a child learns that a toy rattle will make sounds by accident. Once that accidental result occurs, a child learns to make sound by purposely shaking the toy rattle. As a child matures, he or she learns more complex actions and results and even begins to conceptualize and plan for related and similar results. In all cases, however, the child learns that results must be created by some form of self-initiated action.

As a consequence of a child's action-results circular relationship, the child learns to eat, to walk, to talk, to play with friends and to seek pleasant things and to avoid unpleasant things. Later, the child learns to run, to make words into sentences and when to speak and when not to speak. The child learns to do these things and chooses to do these things not because he or she was externally motivated, but because the child internally chose to do those things. That motivation came from within—not as a result of outside pressure, manipulation or a formal motivation seminar.

The choice by many children to continue doing something by themselves to produce natural and desired results is often negated by influences that are contrary to their basic structure. Their natural order is motivation to continue the drive toward enlightenment and fulfillment, but internal influences and external stimuli occur that block those natural inclinations. These negative influences are demotivators.

There are many normal internal and external demotivators that apply to education as well as to any other productivity or self-fulfillment area, such as the workplace. These will be analyzed in the chapter on motivation. It's important in this discussion to acknowledge that a severe and detrimental demotivator in the education process is the blatant and hostile criticism that society generally, and business and political leaders specifically, place on students and teachers. How can students remain motivated to be at their best, and how can teachers continue to teach at their best, when society continues to criticize students and teachers for being unmotivated, incapable and incompetent?

These continuing criticisms, without fact as a basis, are the most damaging demotivators for the education process. If we expect our education process to reach its highest level of efficiency we must begin to recognize, and to express our confidence in, our children and our teachers. To do otherwise is to prevent students and teachers the freedom and the fair opportunity to function and to express themselves in their normal and natural order of self motivation.

Do our leaders and our society have the objectivity and the courage to refrain from self-defensive criticism to avoid pointing the finger of blame at themselves for social and economic failures? If our social problems and our economic problems are to improve, they must have that courage.

School Curricula

There's also much criticism over the choices of courses, or the course requirements that students must complete, particularly in high school. Some critics emphasize that more emphasis should be placed on math and science to help improve our society economically. Others place emphasis on the humanities to help us to understand more as people who need to cooperate in our mixed society. Many place more concern toward the cognitive skills, emphasizing that if students can learn to think correctly they can solve many other problems. There are still others who understand that we must "get back to the basics."

Fundamentally, neither idea is wrong. Students must know how to think logically, they must know how to get along with other people, they must know how to solve problems and they must be reasonably competent in math and science to function in a modern environment. I doubt that anyone would disagree with this general conclusion. If everyone, at least most people, agrees with this conclusion why does the debate remain over the curriculum that a school should teach? Anything positive that a child learns adds value to that child's future, whether it's technical, academic or humanistic.

To repeat a major point that's already been made in this chapter, everything about education remains debatable until a clear purpose for education is established. That includes the content and the value of a school's curriculum. For example, if the purpose of education is determined to be "to develop a more cooperative society," then the humanities should be the courses that are most emphasized. If the purpose of schools is determined to be "to rapidly improve science and technology," then science and math should be stressed more strongly. If the purpose is determined to be "to help each student to develop to his or her full potential," then a more diversified curriculum would be appropriate.

It's inappropriate to criticize or to applaud school curricula that guide our current education system. The validity of each curriculum may be determined if and when the purpose for our education system, or for each facility in the education system, is clearly determined. Anyone who criticizes education curricula at this time hasn't considered all the pertinent factors of the "education dilemma."

Funding For Education

Education is ordinarily discussed on the basis of two broad generalities. One is productivity, which has been the basis of this discussion thus far. The other broad generality that occupies much emphasis and much debate concerns education funding. The major question regarding funding is, "Are we giving enough money into the education process for that process to be effective?"

Research and surveys have concluded that money alone is not the answer to improve education. As in most situations, considering in economic terms, a funding point is reached where there are diminishing returns on expenditures. For example, the first million dollars given into education might gain a million dollars worth of benefit. The second million dollars might gain only half a million dollars worth of benefit. The third million dollars might gain only one quarter of a million dollars worth of benefit. Economically speaking, when the point is reached when there's no gain from more money, the function or the system will be expanded to use that excess money. This absorption of assets, money or time, that has declining value and productivity has been recognized and categorized as "Parkinson's Law." C. Northgate Parkinson, a professor and author, identified that concept.[3]

Nevertheless, adequate funding is necessary to maintain a proper level of education in our society. That efficient level must be determined before a valid decision may be made regarding the adequacy of current funding. This concept is discussed further in the chapter on motivation. Briefly, however, funding must be considered in two dimensions. First is the basic, or maintenance, dimension. Secondly is the enhanced, or motivational, dimension.

The basic dimension should consider the framework of the education system. This would include an organizational structure, school buildings, a required number of school buses, basic teaching equipment, a minimum number of teachers and a basic curriculum. These are the things needed to teach the basic essentials of education, whatever they are determined to be. This basic dimension should be funded even if that means increased taxes.

The enhanced dimension for funding consideration, however, requires a more critical perspective. This would consider those things desired, but not essential to provide a basic level of education. The enhancement dimension would include: extra-curricular activities, teacher aides, a wider selection of course offerings, specialized training and anything else that's not related to providing a basic education to most students. These are some of the things that may provide some motivation to more students, but not necessarily. These are the things, however, that apply directly to "Parkinson's Law."

These are the things that add more dimension to the education process, but there is also less return on the dollar, for each dollar spent. This is assuming of course that the purpose for education is to provide an effective level of social literacy. The importance of funding these items would depend upon the planned purpose for the education process.

How Can Education be Improved?

Finally we come to the last question that was asked at the beginning of this chapter. That question asks how education can be improved. Two equally important and related questions are, "Can education be improved?" and "Do we have the will to take any real action that will improve education?"

There's little doubt that the effectiveness of our education system can be improved. This can occur whether a classroom is furnished with the most modern computers, gadgets and toys; or whether a classroom has nothing more than an old-fashioned teacher who cares for the success of students. A student's interest in learning - and in trying to please a good teacher—is far more important to the learning process than is gadgetry and hands-on philosophy. Our education system possesses the basics, even at this time, to improve educational effectiveness from within.

The education dilemma doesn't lie within the education system. The education dilemma is created in environments external to the education system. The education dilemma is created in weak cultural values of society and lowered expectations in the economic world. Do we have the will, as a country, to improve these conditions to allow the education process to work? We easily have the ability. However, I will not be presumptuous enough to guess if we have the will to use our ability to solve this problem.

Regardless of the efforts, the ability and the will of our generation, we must remain optimistic about the outcome of our society. It's most likely that our young people today will continue to progress and to succeed even with the ambivalence, the obstacles, the discouragement and the criticism that they are forced to endure from society. Their progress and their success would be made easier, however, if we, as a society, decide to develop the will to offer them positive guidance and assistance and a solid foundation for their educational achievements.

The education dilemma, then, is not necessarily or exclusively a problem within the education system. It's a problem largely created by the ambivalence, the self-doubt and the lack of proactive volition by influential members of society and by lower cultures of society.

CHAPTER TWO

EDUCATION AMBIVALENCE

Johnny's parents were both high school graduates. His mother completed one semester of college, then quit to get married and start a job as a desk clerk in a medium-size hotel. His father worked in a distribution company as a shipping clerk. They weren't wealthy, but they considered themselves as part of America's middle class.

Their son, Johnny, was a student in the eleventh grade. Johnny was a marginal student. He passed most of his subjects, but showed little interest in any of his courses. He never studied at home, and he rarely admitted to his parents that he had any homework— that he hadn't completed in school. His parents occasionally asked how he was doing in school, and always looked at his report cards, but outside that interest they assumed that Johnny would graduate and be prepared to enter college.

Johnny knew that he didn't want to go to college when he graduated from high school. He had many friends who found jobs and began work when they graduated. That's what he wanted to do to begin earning his own money to buy a car and to move into his own place. Not only that, Johnny knew that he wasn't smart enough to handle the pressure of competitive grades in college. He knew that would be too difficult for him, since he barely got by in high school. His plan to begin work after high school was based on those two ideas. He wanted to be personally independent, and he felt incapable of surviving four more years of academics.

When classes resumed after the holiday break, at midyear, the counselor scheduled Johnny for an interview to discuss his grades and his career plans. Johnny told the counselor that he wanted to graduate and to begin work at the best job he could find as soon as he graduated. Maybe he could even find a part-time job before he graduated to "get used to the work environment." He told the counselor that he knew he needed his high school diploma to find a good job, for he had always been told that he needed that diploma to be eligible to apply for most jobs.

The counselor, however, knew that Johnny could make better grades, if he would only study and try to make better grades. She also knew that Johnny's mother wanted Johnny to get a college degree to improve his economic possibilities. The counselor tried to convince Johnny that he should work harder to improve his grades to increase his opportunity to be accepted by a college. At the conclusion of the interview Johnny felt belittled and hurt, for he knew that someone would be disappointed with any decision that he eventually made. He knew that he didn't want to go to college and, at the same time, he felt his mother would be disappointed if he wanted to begin a job.

Johnny graduated from high school a little over a year later and began working in a plant that manufactured electronic equipment. He felt unsure and uncertain of his status, however, for he had the feeling that he was disappointing his family. His lowered self-esteem wouldn't allow him objectively and aggressively to become fully interested in his job. Although he learned the technical procedures, easily, he couldn't become emotionally involved with the job. His boss, who assumed that he was a slow learner who had not been trained for a job in high school, often criticized the school system for not preparing students to become good workers. This alienated Johnny from his self-esteem even more, for he felt that his boss didn't have confidence in his abilities.

The Source of Ambivalence

Johnny's situation is only a minor and simple example of the major problem of education caused by the ambiguity and the lack of clarity of the purpose of education. Johnny thought that a high school diploma was only a prerequisite that would qualify him for a job application for a respectable job. Johnny's mother and his counselor felt that Johnny would fail if he didn't utilize his full academic abilities. Johnny's boss thought that the purpose for public school was to prepare a student to be a good technical worker. Johnny became confused and alienated for he felt that he had failed everyone, even himself.

There are many Johnnys and Jonis who face this crisis in our economic and education society. This crisis is created from two sources. First, a clear purpose or clear purposes for public education has not been acknowledged. Secondly, many students who don't desire an advanced academic education are expected to pursue that course to eliminate the appearance of family failure.

This question of the purpose, or the ambivalence, of education is not new. It's a situation that's existed throughout history. The question of the purpose of education extends at least back into the fourth century B.C., with the writings of Plato.[2]

Plato, who developed many of his ideas of life, philosophy, the nature of man and idealism from his study of Socrates, also expressed ideas on the purpose of education. Notwithstanding that Plato believed that the educated elite should also be the chosen idealistic leaders, he also contributed ideas of education for a more universal purpose. He advocated that the purpose of education should be to train a person to look inward to find that person's own goodness. The purpose for finding one's own goodness from within, according to Plato, is to develop a child's innate capacities. This includes the child's ability to appreciate the absolute values of beauty, truth and goodness.

Plato expressed an idealistic philosophy toward education. His idealistic philosophy stressed man's dignity. To develop that dignity to the fullest, Plato felt it was necessary to develop the personality of each individual to its fullest realization of each child. Plato realized that some children had more ability to do that than did other children; consequently, he envisioned higher levels of education only for those who possessed more of that perspective ability. Plato's education concepts did not include JOB SKILLS, career development or college preparation. He was focused on idealism and developing one's inherent nature.

Another opinion expressed later in history was that of Jean-Jacques Rousseau,[2] a writer and philosopher from Geneva, during the mid 1700s. Rousseau was more concerned with nature and freedom. He felt that the purpose for education should be to help people become free and to escape from the chains that ordinarily restrict people's natural tendencies. According to Rousseau, people should be educated according to their nature otherwise they would be masters of no one, not even themselves.

During the founding of our country, our founding fathers had a more personal interest in determining the purpose for education. Thomas Jefferson, and others, focused primarily on ways to sustain the democratic republic that they had visioned and formed. Consequently, their interpretation of the primary goal of education was not to understand ethics and self-expression or to prepare for a career. Their primary vision for the purpose of education was to insure that people learned enough about their government to protect themselves —to become an informed electorate.

Our founding fathers were focused on preserving founding

principles of our country. To them, the most important concept of education was to prevent the encroachment of leaders who would destroy those principles. As Jefferson described the purpose of education, "To teach the young to judge the ambitions and designs of men—to know ambition under every disguise it may assume; and knowing it, to defeat its views."[2] This was not the only purpose cited for education, but at that time it was the major and most emphasized concern.

John Stuart Mill,[2] an English educator during the mid 1800s, emphasized a different purpose for education. He expressed education more in terms of an overall cultural effect than in specific ways to achieve cultural influences. Mill did not necessarily emphasize education for the purpose of career advancement, introspection or intellectual achievements. He merely emphasized that the basic purpose of education is to prepare the current generation to improve to a level that would at least allow that generation to keep up with the past generation. Mill emphasized that each generation should improve culturally, economically and socially from the last generation. If each generation could not improve, education should at least allow that generation to remain at the same level and not decline.

Ellwood Cubberly,[2] another influential educator during the early 1900s, had another important purpose for education for his times. This was during a period of mass immigration into America. People were coming into America from all parts of the world, consequently, they possessed different cultures and different concepts regarding righteousness, law and order and ideas of government.

Cubberly advocated that education should be oriented primarily toward these people. He believed that they should be taught the American way of life—particularly from the Anglo-Saxon point of view regarding culture and righteousness. He believed that assimilation into society with the proper perspectives was more important than preparing for college or preparing for advanced education. Education was considered the vehicle to provide this assimilation.

Later, in the mid 1900s, John Dewey[2] developed a different perspective of education. Dewey was a professor of philosophy at the University of Chicago during this period. Dewey expressed his concern that small village life was breaking down and that society had done nothing to prepare children to cope with more universal social and economic structures in the rapidly changing world.[2]

Dewey advocated a pragmatic approach toward education. He advocated that the primary business of school is to train children to learn how to be more cooperative and mutually helpful in everyday living. He accepted this approach for he believed that the primary root of education is in the instinctive attitudes and activities of children. In this approach, he felt that if children learned to be mutually cooperative to fit into an environment that they would be less concerned with material representations of society. They would be led to success by their cooperative endeavors. Dewey did acknowledge, however, that standardized and structured educational methods would still be required to "fill the gaps."

Dewey's concepts are the basis for the modern and more experimental "progressive schools" that are often discussed in the media. These concepts will be discussed further in another chapter. The purpose here is to simply express that the purposes and aims of education remain ambivalent and confusing.

Modern Ambivalence

The purpose or the primary goal of education remains as confusing to define today as it did during the time of Socrates and Plato. That ambivalence has existed for over two thousand years, and the question still hasn't been resolved.

During modern times, however, the primary purpose for a basic education has been focused toward two possibilities. One of those is to prepare for higher academics—college. The other is to prepare for a vocational or job career. Little concern is given, at this time, for basic education to provide mankind with the ability to find the goodness within himself or herself through a deep introspection into ethics, equality, idealism or morality. Modern focus on education is more pragmatically directed toward personal economic enhancement through academics or vocation. Modern education is more simply directed toward materialism than toward idealism.

Although the focus of education has, at this time, been specifically directed toward materialism, the primary purpose of a basic education still remains ambivalent in practice if not in theory. This is evidenced by the conflict of ideas, conversations and concepts that's perpetuated among well-meaning people who analyze and criticize our education system.

For example, parents, counselors and educators give the impression, by their direct suggestions or innuendo, that the sole purpose for an education is to prepare for higher education—to get a college degree. A student who doesn't conform to this ideology is generally regarded as a failure. Even worse, the student who doesn't conform to this ideology feels that he or she really is a failure. This destroys that student's self-image which is more important to that person's eventual success than the level of education that he or she attains.

Although its recognized that people with advanced education make more money in a lifetime than people with less education, there

Will Clark

are also many successful people who don't have higher educations. Perhaps more of those people who are less academically inclined could be more successful if they are allowed to believe that they can be successful.

Another example of the ambivalence of the purpose of education is the criticism from society, especially business and industrial leaders, that new workers are coming into jobs untrained and unskilled to do those jobs. Their complaint is usually that new workers are not trained in secondary schools to handle the new technology required in the more technological workplace. Their complaint of the education system is based on an unfounded and personally selfish assumption that the purpose of schools is to train their workers. This has never been specified as a basic purpose for schools.

Future Ambivalence

Is it possible to establish a sound and clear purpose for education that will effectively guide future generations? It is, only if one can accurately predict economic and social changes of the future. To understand this concept, it's necessary to examine some possibilities that could, theoretically, occur.

Since the condition of our economy is a major catalyst that determines the nature of many decisions in our society, let's consider some possibilities of educational emphasis and goals based on the economy. These theoretical results may not necessarily be valid, but this analysis will demonstrate how contemporary societal forces determine the emphasis for the perceived purpose of education. Our three examples will include an economy that's very strong and at its maximum capacity, an economy that's adequate but not strong, and an economy that's been devastated to produce despair and anarchy.

Emphasis Within A Strong Economy

During periods of strong industrial and business growth the social emphasis on education would most likely orient toward technology and self-actualization. A growth period fosters greater optimism for society as well as for each person in that society. During this period, productivity is high, incomes are growing and the tax base of society is large enough to care for basic social needs. More importantly, the tax base is large enough to permit more funds to be allocated toward research and development. The economy is able to meet its basic social demands and plan for an optimistic future, simultaneously. It's this anticipation of a better future that will likely

32

place increased educational emphasis on technology that will support more aggressive research and development. Emphasis on research and development will require more advanced concentration on mathematics and sciences. A major part of society, in this case, will most likely focus on technological breakthroughs.

Another major part of society, during periods of high economic optimism, will most likely concentrate on individual self-actualization. This society will be economically comfortable and will, as a result, strive for higher personal goals. That highest personal goal, the highest motivator according to Abraham Maslow[4] is self-actualization. Within this process, people would be more focused on entertainment, sports, arts and other activities that demonstrate their inner nature and deep aspirations and dreams.

These activities are not necessarily money driven. They are more often activities that show an attempt to find personal fulfillment and happiness. This concept and this emphasis may be similar to describe the purpose of education that Plato embraced. That is, to allow a person to become introspective to find the goodness and value within himself (or herself.)

Emphasis Within A Moderate Economy

The accepted purpose for an education in a moderate or stagnate economy might be perceived differently. During those times, education might be considered from three different perspectives. From the perspective of students and parents, an education would be considered as the logical and natural vehicle to develop oneself toward financial security. The emphasis would be on trying to determine the most suitable and the most practical way to avoid economic disaster.

Business leaders would have a different view for the purpose of education. They would most likely rationalize that a higher educated workforce is needed to increase productivity to make their businesses more profitable. In this case, most of the emphasis would be on preparing for job skills, not necessarily for the enhancement of the individual's future. These leaders would not be concerned with individual enhancement or social literacy. They would be concerned with trying to determine how to make their businesses successful.

General society could adopt any popular idea for the purpose of education during a stagnant or moderate economic condition. Society could assume that a more educated population, in any manner, would automatically produce economic success. In this case, it wouldn't matter which approach schools would adopt, as long as more education is the primary goal. Or, society might focus on more vocational and technical training to support the ideas of business and industry. Again, this would be a dilemma between social literacy and job skills as a primary purpose of education.

Emphasis Within A Devastated Economy

It's possible that the primary purpose of education during times of devastation and despair might be oriented more toward the humanities. More educational emphasis might be placed on mutual survival than on technological advancements, wealth-building and self-actualization through higher literacy. Conceivably, educational emphasis would be focused toward concepts of cooperation, fairness, equity, humane treatment, and ethics.

These would be desperate times that would create new situations and new perspectives by most Americans who have never lived in or experienced the conditions of hopelessness, despair and anarchy. Motivations would reorient themselves, and with those different motivations would come different needs to be fulfilled. These new needs, the lower level survival needs, would lessen society's concern for higher level mathematics and sciences and self-actualizing social literacy.

Logically, an exact scenario cannot be forecast in the event of any social or economic change. These examples, above, have not been given to be prophetic. They have been given only as examples to demonstrate that perceptions and emphasis change along with any social or economic change. It can be safely forecast, however, that we will see many social and economic changes in our future.

Understanding the Ambivalence

Education has always had a vague rationality for its existence. Probably no one would deny the importance of education, for without some form of practical education our society would not survive. Education gives people in our society a feeling of adequacy and esteem. It gives them confidence that they are at least somewhat in charge of their lives, since they are capable of understanding most activities and events of society. It also allows them to understand that they are normal within a social structure, and, consequently, may participate in that structure.

Perhaps the concept of education and its purpose will remain ambivalent, for it would certainly be most difficult to devise an education system that would give all things to provide esteem and financial success to all people. Perhaps the most logical way to avoid the ambivalence of education is formally to determine more than one purpose for education. If this were allowed to occur, more people would be encouraged to seek that higher level of esteem and self-confidence that will allow them to become positive contributors to society.

Does our country have the knowledge to remove the ambivalence of the purpose for education? Certainly, for the necessary concepts exist and they are well known. Does our country have the ability and the assets to remove the ambivalence? Yes, for there are many talented people in our country who could accomplish those goals if they were simply allowed and encouraged.

Does our country have the will to remove the ambivalence and to maximize the education process? Probably not at this time. There are too many special interest groups and too many self-serving power struggles in our society to allow a logical and practical transition to an efficient education process that's allowed to function under pure concepts of education. Most education programs are marred by political or specialized social interests. As long as these ambiguous causes continue to invade the education system, the education system cannot become pure to eradicate the ambivalence.

Hopefully, however, most of the ambivalence might be removed by understanding the forces and the causes of that ambivalence.

The purpose of this chapter is to make the causes of that ambivalence known so that it may be recognized and effectively rationalized.

CHAPTER THREE

EDUCATION DISTRACTORS

Our education system, including its philosophies, concepts, people and facilities, has no standard charter or basis in fact to affix, scientifically, a percentage or a ratio to designate its effectiveness. Consequently, the system is completely vulnerable to influential and rhetorical self interests. Much of this rhetorical self interest continues to use education as a base of power building and other selfish interests that harms the value of the system that exists.

Education is used as a political football, an emotional push-button and a social hot potato to achieve ends and results that are not necessarily related to education. Local, state and national politicians target education as one of the major problems of society that must be corrected. Many of those within the education system use the education emotional bandwagon to justify increased pay and benefits. Society, generally, is quick to blame the lack of effective education as the cause of all the major economic and social disasters. All this rhetoric is generated and perpetuated without any evidence that the education system is even remotely related to the problem under consideration.

The Political Football

First, let's analyze the political advantages of a politician at any level to criticize the education system. A politician must have a platform as the basis for a campaign to seek public office. Would it be wise for a candidate, or an aspiring candidate, or one who might consider politics in the future, to suggest that the education system is effective as it exists? This would most likely be an inappropriate action by any candidate who wants to appear knowledgeable, reasonable and capable of solving the many disasters and demons that threaten to destroy mankind.

To have a reasonable political platform, candidates for public office rationally accept the tradition that they must acknowledge or discover the many ills of society that must be corrected. They must also try to convince voters that only they clearly understand those problems sufficiently to determine a corrective course of action. Then they must try to convince voters that only they are capable of making those corrections.

During those political feeding frenzies the validity of the ineffectiveness of the education system is never challenged. It's merely accepted during the emotionalism of arguments and debates that, yes—an education dilemma does exist. The question becomes not whether an education dilemma exists, but, instead, who recognizes it better and who is more qualified to repair the system.

These debates customarily focus on such broad generalities or on such minutia of details that neither argument may be logically substantiated or refuted. For example, some aspirants proclaim that more and better education will improve the economic conditions of that society, locally or nationally. They don't suggest a specific to support that general conclusion. For example, they don't suggest that for every percentage point that the dropout rate decreases there will be a comparable increase in economic conditions. That's merely a generalized assumption.

Another example concerns scholastic aptitude test (SAT) scores. Influential people and special interest people cite those declining SAT scores as the basis of pending economic disaster. There's no basis in fact to prove that a declining national average SAT score of one, two or five points will determine the success of individuals or a society. All those higher test scores, and other test scores as well, prove is that those students taking those tests make higher test scores during any given scoring period. Those test scores don't necessarily prove that the education system was more effective during that cycle.

Evaluative test scores, particularly aptitude test scores, may be influenced by any number of factors other than the education process. For example, according to surveys, test scores of students who are reared and nurtured in a home environment that emphasizes academics will achieve higher scores. Students who are reared in more disenfranchised nurturing environments will most likely score lower on most tests. Of course, there are many exceptions, for many students regardless of their nurturing or social status will possess a higher intelligence level that will allow them to succeed academically, regardless of their environment. That lower cultural environment, however, might restrict those same highly intelligent students from achieving a higher level of social or economic success.

Many of those who rhetorically forecast gloom and doom from declining SAT scores are probably not even aware of the normal and cyclical shifts in SAT scores. Those scores do shift slightly, but there's no evidence to suggest if the shift is caused by educational efforts or other forms of social integration. These scores show normal shifts in SAT scores for the years indicated:

Year	Verbal	Mathematical
1983	425	469
1985	431	475
1987	430	476
1989	427	477
1991	422	475
1992	423	477

Two factors are greatly significant in these scores when they are objectively considered. The first significant factor is that they remain relatively stable. Scores may vary from year to year, but over a long period of time there's only a minimum change.

The second significant factor is that even with a greater increase in marginal students who apply for college, and take the SAT, those test results have not significantly declined. This achievement would suggest that schools are doing an even better job than is realized, for more marginal students who didn't take the SAT in the past are now taking the test—and the average test scores don't reflect those marginal entrants.

Another aspect of SAT scores should also be considered. Those tests measure only a person's basic aptitude to succeed academically. They don't measure a person's drive, ambitions, goals, determination and family and cultural support. It's been suggested that success is approximately sixty percent ability and forty percent action and determination.[5]

This differentiation is important since it establishes a philosophical question as well as a practical question. That question is, "Is the purpose for secondary education to prepare one for higher educational achievements, or is the purpose to prepare one to succeed?" If one assumes that SAT scores are indicators of future success, then many people become perceived as limited in their degree of success based upon their relative SAT scores. This is an unfair and invalid assumption, since those other factors such as determination and cultural background must also be considered as major parts of the success process. If, on the other hand, SAT scores are considered only as potential indicators of one's academic success, then that consideration might be somewhat valid.

Rhetoric condemning our education process and education system has a tendency to create a self-fulfilling prophesy. That prophesy is that our education process is failing. We must consider, however, if our education system is declining or will decline due to events within the system itself, or from the force of negative persuasion by those who continue to practice self-serving rhetoric. This rhetoric continues to distract from emphasis on the good things that our education system is doing, in its attempt to prove that it's an ineffective system that needs to be fixed. The education system is not fairly evaluated before the fixing begins to support a political or other special interest viewpoint.

Economic Purposes

The education system is also used for purposes other than education. The word or the concept "better education" is often a tool used by those within the education system to benefit themselves personally or as an institution. When this call for better education arises the major focus of that better education emphasis is more money to support those persons or those causes.

For example, teacher organizations often claim that the education system will decline and students will not get a "good education" if teachers' pay is not raised to a more professional or equal level. More specifically, these organizations try to compare teachers' pay scales to the quality of education that students are likely to receive. In this comparison, is the quality of education assumed by society to decrease to a lower level if teachers' pay scales are not raised? Are students to assume that they are receiving an inferior, and consequently a useless, education? In this example, is the quality of education more likely to suffer from the lack of higher teacher pay scales or from the distracting rhetoric that attempts to equate pay with quality of education?

Studies and surveys suggest that the level of teacher pay has nothing to do with the quality of education that any student might receive.[1] More likely, the rhetoric that accompanies that argument does more damage to students' perceptions of the value of their educational opportunities. Any perception of personal inferiority would likely lower a student's self-image, thereby negatively affecting those educational results.

Educators often use the "quality of education" tool to request more financial support for their needs and causes. For example, they frequently ask for more classrooms, more equipment and more assistants to help them perform more effectively.

High schools that offer a basic curriculum want to offer more courses. Schools that offer thirty courses want to offer sixty courses. Schools that offer sixty courses want to offer eighty courses. There's constant demand on society in the form of taxes to support these causes.

The fundamental question is, "Are these additional things necessary to provide a basic education that will prepare a student to learn and work, or are these additional things needed by educators to feed their own need for personal esteem and higher status? A more complex organization with more specific demands also creates a higher level of job security by those who are in control of the system.

Whether those who are involved in the education process are sincere in their attempts to improve the education process, or whether their lamentations are ulteriorly designed for their personal gain, those lamentations are distractors that discredit the education process. Educators and administrators must continue to appeal for sufficient funds to maintain an effective level of education for students. However, that appeal should not contain the suggestion that students, at this time, are not being effectively educated. That appeal should be directed at maintaining an effective level of education. With this approach, students and their parents will not be constantly fed the idea that students are receiving an inferior education.

Integration

During the past few decades, racial integration has been one of the major distractors that has disallowed effective emphasis on the education process. Major emphasis has been on trying to insure that classes and schools have a socially acceptable racial mix rather than on trying to insure that each student is given the best environment to receive the best possible education. Educational and social visionaries have been talking out of both sides of their mouths.

The goal of those visionaries is "equality," not equality of opportunity as is often taught. There's a great difference between the concepts of equality and equality of opportunity. A play on words has been used on society to make the move toward social equality more socially acceptable. The fundamental purpose of the strong move toward equality, with schools used as the vehicle for that social endeavor, is to create a larger middle class society. That movement has failed, for now the middle class is declining and there's a larger void between the "haves" and "have nots" than ever before.

Black people, from all indications, seem to have lost more in this social experiment to create equality for them. This especially applies to young black males, who have a higher dropout rate and a higher prison rate. Perhaps if the social experiment had concentrated more on equality of opportunity and less on forced and directed equality, more aspirations of equality might have resulted.

For example, if school classes were divided between more

academically gifted students and less academically gifted students—regardless of race—more emphasis and assistance could be given to those less academically inclined students. Perhaps also, those less academic students wouldn't be intimidated to drop out of school if they were surrounded only by students who were closer in ability and aspirations to themselves. They would be allowed to maintain a sense of self-esteem and dignity. Being forced to compete in a higher strata environment doesn't permit that dignity to exist.

This does not involve a question or an analysis regarding racism and integration. Each unit of an education system based on ability would include members of all races, since academic ability is not limited by race or ethnic background. Academic ability is more often related to cultural background, and there are more poor white people in the United States than there are black people. This analysis is to suggest that the distraction of forced integration by race harmed both white and black students in the education process.

Summary

The quality of education in our country has never been discussed, judged, reviewed or analyzed on the basis of simply the quality of education itself. That analysis is usually clouded and distorted by other factors that have a more personal influence on those who perform that analysis or evaluation.

Recipients and participants in the education process cannot analyze the quality of education objectively, for they have personal interests in that process. Politicians, likewise, have personal interests in the education system that will not allow them to praise that system as it exists. There must be something wrong in that system for them to fix. Society must consider the needs and demands of universal social equity and justice more important than the needs of only one single segment of society—education. These distractors and ulterior motives must be considered in any analysis of the purpose and quality of education in our society.

PART TWO

SUCCESS STRATEGIES FOR THE EDUCATION PROCESS

CHAPTER FOUR

DEVELOPING MOTIVATION

The concepts of motivation are often considered regarding a student's desire and interest to learn. These concepts are important since, obviously, a student who wants to learn tends to be easier to teach; and, that student also stays in school to learn more. The purpose for this chapter is to present motivation principles, ideas and concepts that educators and parents may use to help their students and children become personally motivated. Use of this information may be more valuable than simply trying to force a child to become motivated through threats, intimidation and pleading.

Motivation principles, guidelines and rules are based on motivation theories—not scientific facts. Nevertheless, it's important that these motivation theories be analyzed since these theories are the basis for most motivation thinking and planning.Although motivation theories aren't scientifically based, at the moment these theories are the only tools that leaders, parents and other authority figures have to encourage motivation.

There are three basic motivation theories that are routinely considered. These include the following:

The Hierarchy of Needs Theory—Abraham Maslow
The Motivator-Hygiene (Two-Factor) Theory—Frederick Herzberg
Reinforced Behavior—B.F. Skinner

The Hierarchy of Needs Theory by Abraham Maslow will be analyzed first.

THE HIERARCHY OF NEEDS THEORY(4)

Maslow suggests that motivation, a person's decision to do something, is created when a person has an unfulfilled need. According to this theory, if there were no needs there would be no motivation. Maslow indicates, however, that there are always needs because a new need emerges when one need has been fulfilled.

According to this hierarchy of needs theory, a person's needs have a certain established priority that must be fulfilled, or essentially fulfilled, before another need applies to a person's motivations. Maslow ranks these needs in the following categories and in the following order—the basic need is ranked as number 1, and the highest need is ranked as number 5:

1. Physiological needs
2. Safety and survival needs
3. Belonging
4. Esteem and ego
5. Self-actualization

Although these needs are separate and distinguishable, they may overlap to allow two or more to apply at any given time. They also repeat themselves if conditions repeat to rekindle a previous need. Once a need is fulfilled it's not necessarily permanently fulfilled. These needs will be analyzed:

Physiological Needs

Maslow identifies physiological needs as those things that are necessary to sustain life. This includes food, water, shelter, sex and other things that a person might feel necessary to sustain his or her life. According to this theory, until a person feels that these basic needs are fulfilled other needs are not relevant. For example, it might be unrealistic for a person who's stranded on a bare and isolated island to be concerned about love, belonging and self-actualization if he or she is hungry and thirsty. In this situation, that person would only be concerned about food and water. If food suddenly became available, that person would probably not even be concerned about table manners, which is part of the belonging need environment.

Although this basic need, physiological needs, might be valid in a pure environment, there are too many distortions and alternatives in today's modern society for this need to have a direct application. From a practical viewpoint, there are more rational reasons, excuses and alternatives for a person to avoid direct and motivated action to solve his or her personal physiological needs. The most commonly used rationalization to avoid personal responsibility and personal motivation is that physiological needs should be a social responsibility. Many social, political and bureaucratic systems could not exist without this general rationalization of society.

The word or the concept of motivation is often mentioned regarding its application to children. Parents, teachers and society search for ways to motivate children to take positive actions to become successful. Most often, the emphasis on the basic need, these physiological needs, is used in rational attempts to "motivate" those children.

If Maslow's motivation theory is reasonably valid, and most writings appear to give at least some credence to this theory, then one must conclude that this first level of motivation does not apply to most children. This ineffective attempt by authority persons, parents and teachers, creates frustration for themselves as well as for those children, for their sincere and concerned attempts are usually ignored. Why does this happen? Why are these concerned attempts usually ignored? Why are more despair and frustration created? These questions will be briefly analyzed—in accordance with this theory.

According to Maslow's theory, once a need has been fulfilled it's no longer a real need—or a motivating force. It must be concluded that although children are children, they are still feeling, thinking and rationalizing persons. They are, therefore, also affected by needs. They are, however, not affected or influenced by basic physiological or safety needs. Those basic needs are ordinarily provided by parents—for isn't that the fundamental purpose for parents?

Eventually, those basic needs might influence those children when they are forced by tradition or social pressure to leave home; but while they are children living with providing parents they aren't influenced enough to be motivated by those basic needs. Anticipation of those future basic needs is not as dominant as real needs that exist at the present time. If the need is not the driving force at the time it's not a need.

The first level of motivation for children is normally the need to belong. This is the third level of motivation on Maslow's hierarchal scale. This need will be discussed later.

Safety Needs

The second basic need on Maslow's hierarchy is that of personal safety. Although this need is not a driving or a dominant force in this modern age, it still exists.

These safety needs can easily be represented by castles, moats, drawbridges and walls of ancient history. Today these safety needs are represented by locks on doors, deadbolts, personal canisters of tear gas, stun-guns and hand-guns—with and without permits. Some safety precautions are taken by trying to be prepared for any threat, and some precautions are as simple as avoiding certain neighborhoods or certain sections of the country. The safety need is simply a desire to avoid physical injury.

Belonging

The need to belong is considered by Maslow as the third level, or step, of motivation. It's a generally accepted theory that man is a gregarious creature, and has a need to be with and to feel part of other people in society. This condition is also known as the need for love and affection.

Accordingly, once the first two basic levels of needs are essentially fulfilled, or are no longer dominant, a person begins to be influenced more by the social need, which is the need for belonging. The belonging need may have either a wide or a narrow band of influence.

A wide influence would concern the need to feel a general part of humanity, and to be accepted by society in general. This is the area of self-evaluation by an individual where he or she compares his or her looks, abilities, level of acceptance and communications influence with other expected norms of society.

For example, one might feel that he or she cannot really be an equal member of society because that person feels that his or her looks are less than average in human appeal. Maybe she has red hair, and assumes that she would be more acceptable to society if she had blond hair. Of course, from a practical viewpoint, this problem is easily correctable. There are more serious problems, however. Perhaps a person with a round face assumes that he or she would be happier with a normal narrow face. Perhaps a short person cannot feel a normal part of society because society is assumed to accept people who are average height. Perhaps a person is introverted, withdrawn and shy and doesn't feel that he or she is a normal part of society because normal people in society like to talk to one another. Or, perhaps a person has difficulty with the need to feel part of society because that person feels that his or her skin is the wrong color. These are examples of concerns with belonging needs from a broad perspective.

It should be recalled, from this theory, that the higher motivations cannot be realized until the dominant motivation on the hierarchy is essentially satisfied. Essentially, if a person is preoccupied with his or her unacceptability to society, that person cannot concentrate on the more important motivational needs of personal fulfillment, which is ultimately the need for self-actualization.

The narrow influence of the belonging need takes a different perspective. This need involves one's desire to be accepted by and to be part of a specific reference group. That specific reference group is the one that a person either desires to belong to or that a person thinks that he or she should belong to. The group might be a school group, a work group, a social group, a race group or even a group based on economic status.

If a person observes or imagines common or desirable characteristics within those groups, that person will have a need to feel accepted by those groups. The need to belong, or to feel accepted, doesn't apply to only one specific group. That need can apply to many different groups, simultaneously.

The drive to satisfy the need to belong may produce either positive or negative results. If the person feels closer to a reference group that has low aspirations, then that belonging would most likely have a more negative effect upon a person. In this case, once the person is accepted by that group, that person would be expected to comply with the expected norms and values of that group If that person didn't voluntarily comply with those norms, peer pressure and suggested alienation from the group would tend to bring that person back into acceptable behavior by the group. The reference group is the birthplace of peer pressure. That peer pressure has such force and influence that it can determine, in large degree, if a person will be a success or a failure.

On the other hand, if a person feels more in common with a reference group that's more positive with higher aspirations then that person is more likely to be positively influenced toward success.

Parents and teachers often wonder why children, especially their own children, refuse to be logically motivated. They admonish their children with comments such as these:

> "You've got to get yourself motivated!"
> "Why don't you understand what I'm saying?"
> "Do you want to spend your life in the poorhouse?"
> "Don't you want to get a good job when you go to work?"
> "If you don't make good grades no one will hire you."
> "I just don't know what's going to happen to you!"
> "Why don't you spend more time with your books and less
> time with your friends?"
> "You are really intelligent—why don't you act intelligent?"
> "You are just wasting your abilities."

Of course there are probably occasions when parents or educators have no need to offer these admonitions. It's doubtful, however, if many parents escape this frustrating period of trying to motivate their children.

Maslow's theory gives a clue to understand this frustration by parents who try logically to motivate their children. As briefly stated earlier in this chapter, children have no need to be concerned about the first two levels of motivational needs. Those needs, physiological and safety, are provided automatically by their parents. Ordinary children living with ordinary parents have never been exposed to these needs, therefore they have no motivating influence—they are automatically there.

Parents' and teachers' frustration in this motivational effort occurs because they are trying to influence motivation on the wrong level of needs. They try to encourage motivation of children on the adult's first level of needs, survival, instead of at the child's first level of perceived needs, belonging. This causes the parent to assume that the child doesn't understand what the parent is logically trying to explain. The child probably understands the explanation, but the child is not influenced or driven by a need that's neither pertinent nor timely. Since that logical need is out of place and out of time, it's not a motivator.

Since an unknown need is not a motivator, the motivation of children will most probably continue to be frustrating to parents and educators who try to motivate them by concentrating on the logical basic needs. Most probably, their efforts will get better results if they learn to use the higher level needs of belonging and esteem. The concepts of support, responsibility and status will probably be necessary to achieve this goal. These concepts will be analyzed in more detail during the discussion on demotivation.

Esteem Needs

The next higher need, according to Maslow, is the need or the desire for esteem and other ego-related feelings. Esteem and ego-related needs, along with the belonging need, are considered the social needs. Esteem is the condition of higher status that becomes a motivating influence once the need for a feeling of belonging has basically been fulfilled.

Esteem suggests recognition and respect. That might include recognition and respect that's earned inside the reference group or outside the reference group, but its basis is usually the approval by the reference group. Since reference groups have their own values, principles and norms that are considered acceptable, esteem is usually sought by using those standards as references. If those standards were not understood, as determined by a group, there would be no avenue to develop esteem in the judgement of that reference group.

Self-Actualization (Self-Fulfillment)

Self-actualization is considered the highest level of motivation. According to the theory, it can be achieved only after a person has satisfied the basic motivators, the belonging needs and the esteem needs. After those needs are satisfied, the theory considers that a person is free to do what he or she wants that matches that person's aspirations and self-image.

At this point, a person might fulfill a lifelong dream, make a major contribution to society or become an inspiration to others by being his or her natural self—without basic or selfish motivations. This is the time when a person does something because that person feels that it's his or her major purpose in life—and it's an act that provides major personal satisfaction.

According to the hierarchy of needs theory, most people never reach the level to fulfill self-actualization needs, for they remain at lower levels trying to fulfill those needs. Many people are trying to find a basic job to provide basic needs. Others who have jobs and some security seek belonging, love and affection and may never rise above that level of needs. Still others, maybe most, remain locked into the need hierarchy by trying to find a higher level of esteem and respect that will make themselves feel important. It's rare for an average person to be influenced by a need higher than the esteem need.

Summary

Children, adolescents and students, are not ordinarily influenced by the two basic levels of motivation—physiological and security needs. Parents provide these things automatically, so there's no need for children to concern themselves with these interests. Their first level of needs is the need for a feeling of belongingness and love and affection. They are also concerned by personal esteem within their peer reference groups. Parents who try to reason logically for students to prepare themselves for good jobs in the future, usually use this logic in frustration. That logic represents a future need, not one that's pressing at the moment.

THE MOTIVATOR-HYGIENE THEORY(6)

Frederick Herzberg, another motivation theorist, offered a somewhat different perspective than Maslow regarding motivation influences. Although recognized needs were basically the same, there were two differences in their approaches and recognized influences of those needs. Maslow's motivation theory was a general theory that was intended to apply in the broadest application of motivation. Herzberg's theory was designed primarily for workplace conditions.

The major difference, however, was that Herzberg suggested that some needs were motivators, while other needs were necessary to maintain a level of hygiene, but were not necessarily motivators. According to Herzberg, some leaders were trying to motivate their workers with influences and ideas that were not motivators.

This Two-Factor theory views motivation as having two clearly separate levels. One of those levels includes motivation influences similar to those described by Maslow. Basically, this theory suggests that motivation is created by higher level needs comparable to those esteem needs and self-actualization needs. The following needs are those identified motivators:

Work Itself	Achievement
Growth Potential	Recognition
Responsibility	Advancement

The Two-Factor theory also takes a different approach of these identified motivators. It suggests that when these possibilities are present, a person may be motivated—but when these possibilities are not present, a person will not necessarily be demotivated. They are positive when they are present, but they aren't necessarily negative when they aren't present.

The second factor in Herzberg's theory is the maintenance, or hygiene, factor. Accordingly, to maintain a reasonable level of motivation certain factors must be present. If these factors are not present to maintain that level of "hygiene," people in that environment will suffer negative motivation. These hygiene factors include:

Reasonable Policies	Good Supervision
Acceptable Peers	Working Conditions
Fair Salary	Job Security
Personal Life	Good Relations

According to Herzberg's theory, if these conditions are not present workers will suffer from lack of hygiene that will cause them to be unmotivated. If these conditions are present, however, they will have no significantly positive effect on motivation.

To briefly summarize, Herzberg suggests the following concerning motivators and hygiene factors:

> Motivators: Allow a person to become motivated when the possibility of achieving these factors exists, but they do not cause demotivation if they don't exist.

> Hygiene Factors: Cause a person to be demotivated if they do not exist, but don't create a condition for motivation when they exist.

School Environments:

This hygiene concept may apply to environments other than work environments, although Herzberg didn't expound it to wider application. In our modern world, it's becoming clearer that this hygiene concept could apply very well to education.

For example, to preclude students from becoming demotivated, it wouldn't be unreasonable for students—as well as their parents—to expect the following hygiene levels in their schools that would require:

- School systems that understand their purpose
- Political views that universally support education
- Stability in educational leadership
- Student priority rather than system priority
- Professional and caring teachers
- Elimination of distractions—good discipline
- Respect among peer students
- A comfortable and pleasing environment

These are the basic fundamentals that must exist in a school environment to meet the normal expectations of anyone going to school. These fundamentals would not necessarily create or enhance student motivation, but they would certainly create a basic environment where students could become motivated based on other motivational factors. The absence of these basic fundamentals—hygiene —is probably a key to the major problem of trying to motivate students. The question might not be how can students be motivated, the more applicable question might be do fundamental conditions allow students to become motivated?

This hygiene concept, related to motivation, could apply to family environments, as well. Aren't there certain fundamental conditions that family members expect within their households? For example, aren't the following minimum conditions reasonably expected to exist within family environments:

- Protective and supportive parents
- Parents who set good examples for children
- Parents who provide survival needs
- Parents who care about their child's feelings
- Parents who take time to listen to children
- Parents who display self-respect
- Parents who respect and care for each other
- Parents who treat children as people
- Children who are disciplined and courteous
- Siblings who support each other
- An environment that provides comfort

Many of these conditions have been casually discussed during conversations pertaining to education and motivation. However, these factors have never been formed into a clear and usable theory that might be seriously considered to develop a definite plan to improve the education environment.

WHAT IF?

What if we renamed this theory the Educational Motivation Theory? What would be the motivators and hygiene factors under this new theory? Let's explore.

Typical motivators might be: meaningful work, esteem, opportunity, recognition and responsibility. These motivators seem familiar, don't they?

Hygiene factors might be: A good school environment, fair and equitable treatment by teachers, freedom from oppression by peers, competent leadership and administration, a feeling of personal security, and a supportive and secure home environment. These are also appropriately similar to workplace hygiene factors.

The essence of this theory suggests that the motivators cannot have desired effects until the hygiene factors are satisfied to create an acceptable level of emotional maintenance. Historically, and traditionally, all the emphasis has been applied toward the motivators without first developing a reasonable level of hygiene to maintain those motivators.

In effect, students aren't allowed to have good emotional and psychological health toward education, their work, because society not only fails to resolve these hygiene factors—society also refuses to allow students to have most of the motivators. Two of those factors will be used as examples of this social motivation weakness:

1. Why aren't high school students required to teach or tutor lower grade students—at least one hour daily? Would that not fulfill all the motivators described above? It would certainly be meaningful work and it would give esteem and recognition.

2. Why isn't more emphasis placed on emotionally safe, secure and supportive environments than on directly trying to improve testing and evaluation of students? Can students improve themselves in an environment that's not conducive to improvement? This includes home environments as well as school environments.

These are only two questions from this motivation concept. Many more may easily be asked, but these examples are sufficient to suggest that we must generate more questioning attitudes if we hope to help students to develop their inherent abilities. We must also accept students as real and rational people with meaningful thoughts and abilities.

Age probably has little to do with basic and innate intelligence. Students must be allowed, encouraged and supported to use their intellectual abilities to maintain a reasonable level of emotional and psychological health.

BEHAVIORAL CONDITIONING (OPERANT CONDITIONING)

During the 1930s, B. F. Skinner, a behaviorist in the United States, along with counterparts in Europe, introduced and described a learning and conditioning concept that they termed operant conditioning.[7] By their definition, operant conditioning applies to voluntary behavior, as contrasted to classical, or respondent, behavior that refers to reflexes.

Respondent behavior, according to their definition, results from a specific stimulus such as salivating in anticipation of eating food. Operant behavior, on the other hand, is described as occurring spontaneously from the subject—person or animal—within an environment. The difference is that operant behavior involves a choice that may be made from different alternatives. It's not an automatic reflex, as is the case with respondent behavior.

Basically, classical behavior is behavior that's in reaction to a physiological response, such as salivating in anticipation of food, increasing of a pulse rate when frightened, or going to sleep when one cannot stay awake. Operant behavior is that behavior in an environment that allows a person to make an obvious choice of actions such as: which sweater to wear, how to tie one's shoes, which movie to watch, which food to eat when one is hungry—and whether or not to study. Classical behavior is more internal and operant behavior is more environmental. Operant behavior considers a matter of making choices and decisions.

How Does Operant Behavior Affect Motivation?

Operant behavior is identified and described under the general classifications of learning and cognition. It's not identified specifically as a classification of motivation. However, since the concept of operant behavior, as identified by Skinner, includes the concepts of options and voluntary choices, those options and choices must be made to satisfy some needs. If those choices are need motivated, then it would seem reasonable to consider operant behavior also in the classification of motivation. Behavior would suggest action, and action would suggest an activity to reach some satisfaction.

Operant conditioning suggests that actions that result in something that's liked will probably be repeated. Actions that result in something that's not liked will probably not be repeated. This cause and effect reaction is regarded as conditioning by rewards and punishment. Its repetition is considered reinforcement to that behavior. If the result is a reward, the action is likely to be repeated. If the result is a punishment, the action is less likely to be repeated.

According to this theory, reinforcement may be either positive reinforcement or negative reinforcement. Actions that are increased to gain more rewards are considered as positive reinforcement. Those actions that are increased to avoid punishments are considered negative reinforcement. A cause and effect condition, whether real or not, may cause unusual behavior and actions by an individual. For example, it may cause a condition of superstition.

How does operant conditioning apply to education? Is it currently used and is it used effectively? Let's examine these important questions, briefly.

Operant conditioning may be an effective tool in the motivation process for students. It's attempted in many classrooms and families, but its effects are usually only short-lived. This occurs because the concept is ordinarily changed from an operant conditioning concept to a more direct rewards and punishment concept. There are important subtle differences between these two concepts that must be understood to allow an educator or a parent to use operant conditioning effectively.

Ordinarily, in a rewards and punishment concept the student, or other subject, knows the rewards or the punishment to be earned upon the conclusion of a known event. For example, in a grammar school classroom a student who does well on an assignment anticipates that he or she will receive a gold star on that assignment. The gold star is a reward for that good performance, but it's not operant conditioning for it's not leading the student in a general direction of higher performance. Ordinarily, if the student doesn't receive the gold star for each good performance, the student becomes disappointed and demotivated. Under operant conditioning, the student would be given higher rewards at random intervals for increased performance. Under this concept, the reward would not be an anticipation, and the recognition would tend to keep the student internally programed for improvement—not necessarily on remaining on the same level.

A common example of the difference between rewards and punishment and operant conditioning may also be used for family environments. Parents often try to motivate their children toward good grades and educational achievement by offering specific rewards for good grades and good conduct. In this case money is commonly used for that motivator. The parent offers to give the child a certain sum for each high grade earned on his or her report card at the end of each reporting period. Under this concept, earned money is the positive motivator and the lack of earned money is the negative motivator.

This reward and punishment concept by parents ordinarily fails to condition a child toward consistently positive behavior. This failure is caused by two fundamental problems.

First, the child is not subjected to a subtle reinforcement of cause and effect. The reward should be as a result of good performance—not as a result of a promise to reward good results. The rewards should also be random, but often enough to establish a growing internal anticipation that creates reinforcement to continue that activity.

Secondly, one of a parent's roles is to provide security and material necessities for their children. According to the analysis of Maslow's theory, above, children are not ordinarily motivated by those things that parents should automatically provide for them. This includes comfort and material necessities.

The differentiation between material necessities and desires often becomes so obscured that those desired items are perceived by children as necessities. Herzberg's concept of hygiene must also be considered in this situation. A child should not be promised something special if that reward might be considered as part of that child's normal condition of hygiene.

Operant conditioning should be considered as one of the logical ways to motivate students and children to be more successful in the education process. Before an educator or a parent specifically attempts to use a program of operant conditioning, however, the subtleties and differentiations of this motivation concept must be understood. Otherwise, it might be confusing for the student and frustrating for the educator or parent.

PERSONALITY-BASED MOTIVATION

Is it possible that people take actions on the basis of considerations other than motivation theories? The concept that formal theories are merely theories and not scientific facts permits this consideration to be a reasonable possibility. Some personality traits that might be possible causes of motivated actions include the following:

- An inherent desire for knowledge
- Curiosity
- Obligations
- Responsibility
- Character traits
- Jealousy
- Revenge

There are no studies that suggest that these traits and characteristics apply directly toward motivated actions. However, we cannot ignore the possibility that if these traits can be developed into positive characteristics of a person, that person might increase his or her own internal motivation to satisfy needs generated by these traits.

SUMMARY

These motivation theories, concepts and ideas have been offered for only what they are: theories, concepts and ideas. Factual instructions for motivation cannot be presented, for none of those exist.

Although these theories are not factually-based, they are nevertheless all that we have to use at this time. There are many indications that suggest that many of these theories and ideas do work when used in the proper way, at the proper time and in the proper place. This proper application could reasonably be identified as situational motivation.

A major factor remains dominant in the process or the act of motivation. That is, the person doing, or trying to do, the motivating of another person must be of high character and must be respected by the person who is to be motivated.

What can we as leaders, educators and parents really do to improve student motivation? Why not simply create good education hygiene, and then ASK STUDENTS what would allow them to motivate themselves. They have brains that allow logic, if tasked meaningfully. Should we not allow students the opportunity, the recognition, the esteem, the responsibility and the meaningful work to participate. Are those not the same things that we as responsible adults want?

CHAPTER FIVE

A PURPOSE FOR EDUCATION

Vast amounts of effort, energy and time are wasted on ineffective attempts to improve education for students. This waste results from two principles:

First, is the fundamental question regarding a definition of the purpose of an education. Until that important question is answered, education cannot be significantly improved. Any effort to improve the education system without first defining the purpose of education is similar to throwing darts without a dart board. It's literally impossible to hit the target.

Secondly, is a management concept called "Parkinson's Law." [3] Parkinson's Law basically suggests that work expands so as to fill the time available for its completion. There need be little or no relationship between the work to be done and the size of the staff to do it, especially paperwork. The law of multiplication takes over, for when one has too much to do, that person requests multiple subordinates, not a co-worker. As a result, ineffective and unnecessary bureaucracies are formed to serve themselves, not the needs of the original purpose. The educational dilemma question has positioned self-serving bureaucracies that serve no purpose in education other than to absorb budgets that should be targeted directly at education needs. Any increased education budgets will most probably be absorbed by larger bureaucracies to comply with "Parkinson's Law."

To improve education, if that's indeed a reasonable consideration, the purpose for education must be clearly defined. Below are some possible definitions of the purpose of education that show the complexity of this question:

- To accumulate enough information and confidence within oneself to become a person who's comfortable interacting in society

- To gain background information and specific information that will be useful to help one succeed in a chosen career
- To prepare a person to enter college to develop a professional career
- To learn to study and make good grades
- To force assimilation to prevent psychological voids between different cultural and economic groups
- To learn how to succeed

Each of these possibilities could be the subject of debate that could occupy volumes of writings. For examples, two possible purposes of education will be considered. These examples will be: education as a basic source of learning to integrate socially, and planning to succeed.

Social Integration and Assimilation

Throughout recorded history the question of mankind understanding itself has been at the forefront of philosophy and education. This question continues on an individual level for each person. That question remains, "What's the purpose for my existence?" Philosophers and educators attempt to answer this question in the form of great writings and in the form of an education process. This question has never been answered to satisfy the curiosity of every individual, and perhaps that task is even impossible.

The same fundamental question continues to exist for our society as well as for each individual in our society. That question is, "What's the purpose for our society?" Possible answers to this question are offered from a wide range of logical alternatives. This wide range or spectrum of possible truths to that answer includes from inalienable rights for each person on one end of that continuum, to the maximum benefit of society on the other end of that continuum. Answers and solutions are sought within that limited range of possibilities. For education to be truly effective, it must be conducted in consonance with that answer.

At one end of that continuum is the purpose of social integration. Just this one single purpose alone, however, creates complicated questions within itself—and this is only one small part of the possibilities on that continuum, or that range of possibilities Let's step inside only that one small part to help understand the complexity of the complete question.

Social integration has concerned mankind throughout history and throughout all parts of the world. Before we continue with the analysis of social integration as a purpose for education, it's important that the concept of social integration be differentiated from the concepts of cultural and ethnic integration. Otherwise, this analysis might be somewhat confusing.

Social integration, for the purposes of this analysis, should be considered as becoming adapted to fit the mores, values and economic principles of an identified society. This would mean that members of that society would learn to live by the same rules, the same moral expectations and the same economic anticipations of the leaders of that society that establish accepted policies. For example, they would have the same opinions on crime, fairness, equity, rights and the value of personal effort.

Cultural or ethnic integration would be important to certain identifiable groups within the social system. These groups would have their own interests and agenda; however, those interests would fit within the expectations of the social system of which they are a part. Cultural and ethnic concerns would most likely involve ideas regarding heritage, beliefs, ethics and morals. The higher and overriding social order would be more concerned with fairness, equity and protection of rights. Historically, many cultural and ethnic forces conflict. Within a society, those conflicts that tend to disrupt that society must be subjugated for the benefit of that society. This subjugation, or this assimilation, is the task of social integration. That is, to bring everyone into the normal range of social expectations to allow them to understand their rights, expectations and opportunities within that society; and to understand that others within that society share those same rights and responsibilities.

Now, assuming that social integration is the established purpose for education, how would the education system be organized to accomplish that purpose? Let's examine a theoretical school that might be designed for that purpose.

This school would most likely be designed with a stronger emphasis on communications, humanities, geopolitics, agri-business and philosophy. Mathematics and sciences would be taught, but only at the lowest level to allow everyone to share the same level of knowledge and inner experience. Higher level technical courses would form an invisible barrier that might alienate the less academic student from shared and mutual involvement with the education and social process. This alienation might negatively affect that assimilation process.

More emphasis might be focused toward group and social achievement than on individual personal success; consequently, individuals would be encouraged to comply with the consensus of groups. Basically, class courses might be designed more to promote an orderly and cooperative society than on personal success by each individual. Theme words that might be dominant in this education environment might be: equality, fairness, rights, justice and economic parity.

Under this agenda, the education system would be concerned with preserving the society through compromise, not on advancing the society through progressive planning. Progressive planning for individual success would be on the other end of that continuum to determine the purpose for education. That will be considered next.

Learning to Succeed—An Education Purpose

If learning to succeed were to be the chosen purpose for education, then the education system must be restructured for that defined purpose—through organizational and conceptual simplicity. Success is a simple process that shouldn't be confused by, and made complex by, a disoriented and ambivalent education process.

An education system designed for maximum student success might be organized as follows:

1. All students would be required to attend basic social-building education and literacy classes through what is the traditional eighth grade.

2. Assigned scores (grades) through the eighth grade would be "advance" and "pass." Both grades would permit a student to accelerate to the next level without the haunting stigma of a sub-level grade. "Advance" would indicate that the student exhibited good studentship and social skills. "Pass" would indicate that the student is qualified, but shows no interest in active studentship. Failing students would not receive a grade. They would remain at the same level until they could achieve at least a "pass" grade. The "pass" grade could occur anytime during the school year to offer incentive and positive support to those students who had not "passed" at the end of the eighth year.

3. A significant difference would occur at the ninth grade level. At this level, students should have a choice. That choice should be either a career education or a professional education. Those students who were rated "advance" should be automatically accepted into the professional education school. Those students who were rated "pass" should be permitted into the professional educational program only under strict guidelines. Those guidelines should require the student to pass a basic literacy test and to acknowledge that violations of discipline or

good studentship will result in exclusion from the professional program. Students in the professional education schools would be preparing for college; therefore, the standard grading system would apply.

4. Students with a "pass" grade, with the exception above, would attend a four-year career education course. This course would continue the basic social-building and literacy courses, and would include equal time for career training and specific job training courses in the craft and trade skills, as well as administrative and clerical skills. Students in the primary system who had not "passed" by their sixteenth birthday would automatically transfer to the career development school. The standard length of the career development school would be four years, without specifying a grade level. At the end of the fourth year, students would be graded "completed" or "completed with honors."

5. With agreement between the school and students, students may remain in the career development school more than four years. This exception would be to develop a slow learner, to build additional skills, or to assist in training other students while seeking a job. The career development schools would be open to any person, regardless of age; so long as the purpose of the training is to develop or enhance a career—not to learn a hobby.

6. Students in the career development school would be permitted to transfer to the professional education school upon the following criteria:

   - They must pass a standard literacy test
   - They must be recommended by the career school
   - They must agree to good studentship principles
   - The parents must agree to assist the student

Advantages of the Success Concept

This briefly defined concept, above, would incorporate many success principles. During the initial years, grades one through eight, students in the lower half of the class would not be labeled by their peers as failures. Most importantly, they would not consider themselves as moderate to severe failures. Generally, everyone could feel equally important. Dale Carnegie advises[8], "Let the other man save face."

Children don't ask, nor do they deserve, to be thrown into a vicious arena of esteem-destroying comparison. Is there really any need to assign a grade to a student that indicates he or she is "more stupid" than other children?

After the eighth grade, students could begin to have some influence over their own lives. They could have a choice of participating in a graded comparative process through the professional development schools, or by entering a more direct and easily understandable career training program. Why should students be forced into a professional development curriculum that they resent, and most probably will not use?

This freedom to choose a less stressful, more career-oriented approach would permit more marginal students to have full personal esteem. That esteem would encourage them to continue their educations, and not drop out of school to enter the ranks of the chronically unemployable.

Student disciplinary problems would be eliminated, or at least reduced, in the professional development schools. This would allow that educational process to be enforced, for those students would not be distracted and annoyed by those other students who realize that they have no practical reason for a professional education. School curricula may be upgraded, for there would be no need to design classes to allow accomplishment by those less inspired students. The real education system could be upgraded to meet future demands of the professions.

The career development schools would also upgrade skills in general society. Unskilled adults would have a common source for developing skills to begin a career ladder. The common man, and woman, in society would have an avenue to find personal self-esteem which is the first building block of success.

No one would be excluded from either success ladder. The less inspired, however, must show their desire to participate in the professional academic program—with support by their families— before they are permitted to enter that program. They should not be permitted into that program if they have shown a continued history of disruption, inability or lack of good studentship.

Everyone is allowed to maintain his or her dignity and personal esteem, without comparative judgements; and have a clear path to personal success at the same time. Without grades, one can learn to feel as successful as anyone else, for he or she is not labeled as a failure—before life actually begins.

Summary—Two Examples

These two examples present scenarios that show the complexity of establishing the purpose of an education. Even these brief examples suggest that any considered purpose could occupy volumes of writings and years of debate. Adding to this complexity is the fact that there are many possible reasons, or purposes, for an education. Regardless of the actual purpose for an education, if a purpose is ever established, it must be designed to allow, encourage and demand personal success by every student.

The student with less intelligence and ability must be allowed to achieve the same degree of feelings of success as the student with the highest intelligence and ability. If not, then school systems are designed to generate more failures than successes. For a student to become successful, that student must constantly be treated and respected as successful. THE CURRENT EDUCATION SYSTEM DOES NOT ALLOW THIS CONDITION FOR EVERY STUDENT.

CHAPTER SIX

NEW VISIONS

The previous chapter analyzed the importance of defining and establishing a recognized purpose for education before it would be possible to achieve a condition of maximum effectiveness in the education process. An earlier chapter, in Part One, suggested that it might be difficult to establish a fixed purpose for education, since social and economic conditions and emphasis often change. These frequent changes constantly create new perceptions to question the purpose for education at any given point in time.

Regardless of our ability or inability to determine the fundamental purpose for education, the education process must become more effective even within those known limitations. Notwithstanding that the education process might be more directly efficient if all known variables could be considered, that doesn't suggest that the education process cannot become more effective even within these limitations. Even with these limitations the results of the education process can be improved. The current education establishment, however, needs to take a more universal perspective to make that improvement.

That new perspective requires educators and administrators to focus more on developing a more confident and adaptable student rather than a specifically educated and trained student. Students must be prepared to anticipate changes, transitions and new challenges. That education emphasis must be focused toward four new areas that will accomplish that goal. Those four areas include: how to learn, communications and comprehension, developing self-image and confidence and general skills.

It's also important to remember, while we analyze these four concepts, that these concepts apply primarily to students who don't know how to use their innate abilities. High achieving students will likely continue to be high achieving students regardless of this new emphasis, for there continues to be many high achieving students in any education environment. The purposes for these new approaches are to increase the number of high achieving students and to give new optimism to those lower students who don't succeed, from their self-doubt and feelings of inferiority. These four new approaches to accomplish these goals will be analyzed next.

Learning How to Learn

Learning to learn is a subject that's almost ignored in most schools—and is totally ignored in others. Our current education system seems to take the approach that if information is fed into empty shells (brains) and then reinforced by feedback through the evaluation and testing process, that learning will automatically occur. Obviously, this assumption has been used for generations even though its not been proven to be a valid assumption. This false assumption, or lack of a more effective assumption, has permitted the teaching and learning process to remain less effective. More simply stated, if we want students to learn something that's worth learning then we should teach them how to learn. Our education system has ignored this important first step to the learning process.

An example that demonstrates the importance of learning to learn in the education process is the concept of learning to teach in the education process. Teachers are not only taught their subject specialties such as mathematics, science and economics; they are also taught how to teach. They are given the basic information and they are taught how to convey that basic information during the education process.

Students, however, are usually given only the basic information. They are not taught how to receive, or to accept, that basic information—or even what to do with it when they do understand how to receive it. They often don't understand the receiving process or the relevance of the information to real world application.

To resolve this problem, schools must teach a basic study skills course. There are some schools, and some classrooms, that attempt to do this, however, those attempts are unorganized. Study skills are casually encouraged by some teachers, but a study skills program doesn't exist to demonstrate the importance of really knowing how to learn. Well-meaning educators discuss the learning process only as they have time during their busy schedules, or as they happen to think of an important idea to help a desperate student or parent. Those specific study skills are detailed in Part Three which offers direct guidance to help students and parents in the education process.

Students must not only be taught how to learn, they must also be taught how to use new knowledge when they learn it. The second fundamental education need, communications and comprehension, must be taught to help students learn what to do with that new learning. That need will be reviewed next.

Communications and Comprehension

The ability to communicate effectively is one of the major determinants of success for most people. The ability to comprehend and understand related concepts through active cognition is another of the determinants to individual success. Although these two traits are related, since they both involve mental and psychological interactions, they will be discussed separately for clarity and simplicity.

Communications

To learn, to learn how to learn, and to use what one has learned require the effective use of communications. Schools are apparently somewhat aware of the importance of the communications process, for they ordinarily conduct courses on the basic elements of communications. These courses usually include the proper use of grammar, basic appreciation of prose and poetry and a few short speeches in the classroom. Although these standard courses are essential to teach those basic element of communications, they aren't sufficient to teach the full scope of communications that's required to help a student become successful.

Schools must also teach students how to use that basic knowledge of the communication fundamentals. Students are taught the "what" of communications, but they ordinarily are not taught the "how" of communications. There's a significant difference in these approaches. The "what" provides the tool. The "how" demonstrates how to use the tool.

One might ask, "Why should schools be tasked to teach students how to communicate once they have been given the fundamental knowledge? Shouldn't they learn that process during their social interactions and within their family environments?" The answer to these questions are self-evident when it's recalled that this guidance doesn't apply to those upper goal-directed and naturally successful students. This progressive approach is intended to help those students with less ability, and with less opportunity, to learn how to become successful. Those naturally gifted and inspired students would likely succeed despite the weaknesses of any education system.

Other students, those with less ability and less opportunity, need a different approach to learn effective communications. The actual use of communications, regardless of the knowledge of the communications process, is influenced more in the home environment and the cultural environment of a child than in the artificial environment of the education process. Even when a child takes the knowledge of an effective communications process into his or her home or cultural environment that knowledge is not used or reinforced by practice and usage. The culture of the child's environment is stronger than the knowledge learned in the education system. That use and reinforcement must be learned and practiced in the school environment so strongly that that positive environment will have more influence than the more negative environment of the child's culture.

Our analysis, so far, has focused on the reason for the need to teach an active and meaningful communications process in secondary schools. That need, simply stated, is to provide an alternative cultural environment that will allow disadvantaged students an opportunity to practice and reinforce the communications process they are taught. The goal of this process is to make the school environment more dominant than the student's normal negative cultural environment.

Once this goal becomes clear, the process to fill that goal becomes somewhat easy to formulate. A course titled Active Communications should be established and required for each school year, probably beginning in the sixth grade. This course could be somewhat flexible in content, but would fulfill at least those essentials identified below.

All students must:

- Participate in casual group conversations
- Participate in formal group assignments
- Learn to lead group discussions
- Learn how to tell jokes and anecdotes
- Learn how to summarize a group discussion
- Learn how to initiate a conversation
- Learn to communicate with different age groups
- Learn how to criticize positively
- Learn how to accept criticism
- Learn how to speak extemporaneously
- Learn how to be poised when speaking
- Learn how to debate and negotiate

The overriding purpose of this course is to allow a student, over a long period of time, to develop inherent self-confidence in his or her abilities to be part of society, and not merely part of a narrow culture. Image and self-esteem are the ultimate goals of this process. With enough self-esteem, a student from a lower culture in society is not handicapped by that culture. The student learns during the Active Communications class that he or she is as intelligent and as worthy as all other students, regardless of social or economic status. Berelson and Steiner, human behaviorists, define this culturally handicapped condition as narrow personality.[9]

Two things are critical to enhance the effectiveness of this class. First, the teacher must be one who earns respect and admiration from students. A teacher who's disinterested or who cannot empathize with distressed students will destroy the effectiveness of the class. Secondly, a grading system should not be relevant to this class. The question should be, "Can this student communicate well and comfortably in general society," not "Has this student earned an "A" or an "F."

Another consideration would make this class even more meaningful and effective. People in the business community should be part of this classroom interaction—not necessarily in the role of teacher or advisor—but in the role of a mutual participant. This would help to eliminate the belief by culturally deprived students that other normal people in business and society are significantly different in basic abilities and intelligence. The fundamental purpose for this class is cultural assimilation into the expected norms of society.

Comprehension

Comprehension, which is one of the cognitive skills, cannot be isolated for separate training. Consequently, it should logically be taught and reinforced in the Active Communications class. The other cognitive skills may be identified as assimilation and conceptualization. This analysis will consider only comprehension, for those other cognitive skills might result from increased comprehension—it's not certain that they can be taught.

The agenda of the Active Communications class is to train reluctant students, probably by strong encouragement at first, to understand and emotionally to feel that they have minds and real intelligence that can be activated to function on the same level as anyone else in society. When they are forced into the mini-society of the Active Communications classroom they will not have an opportunity to remain locked within that narrow personality that Berelson and Steiner describe. They will be forced by class participation to expand that personality.

When that narrow personality becomes expanded it must be occupied by something. That something is increased comprehension.

Once comprehension is increased within these culturally or emotionally deprived students, they are then able to develop meaningful confidence and self-esteem. This becomes the basis for each individual's success.

That confidence and self-esteem must be encouraged and reinforced by understanding the success process. That will be introduced next and is identified as success planning. Success planning should also be taught as part of the normal school curriculum—in a formal classroom.

Success Planning

Many people assume that success either happens or it doesn't happen for a person. That might happen to a few people, but it happens so infrequently that that accidental event cannot be planned as a basis for a successful future. Ordinarily one must plan to be successful to really be successful. Norman Vincent Peale once wrote, "You can be greater than anything that can happen to you." [10] Success planning is based on that concept.

The action of becoming successful must be a planned event. In the normal process of planning, things and actions must be considered and planned. Once they are planned, they must then be done. Success planning includes consideration of the following events and activities:

1. Understanding goals
2. Developing a successful attitude (DASA)
3. Avoiding demotivation (Determination)
4. Self-development
5. Avoiding frustration
6. Improving communications skills
7. Improving interpersonal relationships

These are the simple success planning factors or elements that are often identified as "the secrets of success." Since we no longer want them to be "secrets" we should understand the simplicity of each of these topics. Each of these secrets, except "avoiding demotivation," will be discussed next. Although the topic of avoiding demotivation will be discussed in Part Three, it remains part of this class curriculum on success planning.

Understanding Goals

Success is determined by accomplishing goals. If a person doesn't assign himself or herself goals then that person cannot accomplish those goals. Instead of having a plan for success, one will have a definite plan for failure. A misunderstanding of goals, however, may also cause failure. Students are often advised by parents, teachers or other authority figures to assign goals to themselves, but many aren't able to do that clearly enough to establish a target for success. Understanding goals is important in the process of assigning goals to oneself, for one might think that he or she has assigned a goal when, in fact, that person hasn't assigned a goal.

Goals may be identified by two types and two dimensions. The two clearly identifiable types of goals include short-term goals and long-term goals. This concept of short-term and long-term goals seems simple enough, but many people fail to become successful because they don't understand the implication of the relationship between these two types of goals.

Short-term goals must be set to accomplish long-term goals. Too often a person assigns himself or herself a long-term goal that's so distant that it becomes unreachable. Those long-term goals are reached by assigning and reaching a series of short-term goals. Not only must long-term goals be reached by accomplishing short-term goals, the reinforcement of success by accomplishing each of those short-term goals makes the possibility of reaching the long-term goal a reality. The success process is learned through achieving short-term goals. The long-term goal evolves naturally. This concept could be called "The magic of little wins."

Successfully achieving long-term goals is determined by achieving a series of short-term goals. If it's that simple, why isn't it easy for everyone to become successful? It is easy for everyone to become successful - there's usually one major problem, however. That major problem is the fear or the unwillingness to take the first step to accomplish the first short-term goal. Most unsuccessful people fail to take that first simple step. Let's examine some simple, yet common, examples of planning for college.

Many high school graduates plan to get a college degree; however, only a few actually follow through to reach that goal. The difference in whether a person gets a college degree is not usually determined by desire, by cost, by need or by intelligence. That success is more often determined by the simple fact that some graduates assign a short-term goal of going to the college to enroll. Others only plan to go to the college to enroll—someday.

Another reason that some high school graduates don't get their college degree is that they can't wait to get the degree. Each individual course is considered an insurmountable obstacle rather than a short-term goal. Those who fail focus on the long-term dream and not the realistic short-term goals of each individual course.

Although understanding the differences and inferences of short-term goals and long-term goals is important, there are other equally important considerations of goals. These include the dimensions of definite and indefinite goals.

Often a person will think he or she has assigned himself or herself a goal when, in fact, that hasn't occurred. That person might have assigned an indefinite goal which is really not an attainable goal. The two important dimensions of goals include the definite and the indefinite.

A definite goal is one that may be clearly described, identified and achieved, or reached. It's also one that may be measured in degrees of completion along the way.

For example, how many times have you heard someone say, "My goal in life is to save enough money to retire on when I get old, so I can live happily ever after?" This common statement, belief or anticipation is a primary cause of failure for many people who would like to succeed in life. There's a fundamental flaw with this goal, however, that makes it unreachable. That fundamental flaw is the fact that this isn't really a goal. It cannot be measured, and it cannot be understood if it's reached. Two concepts make this goal unachievable.

First, many people never feel that they are old. At what age would this person consider as the right age for that goal? Secondly, the exact amount of money needed for retirement hasn't been specifically stated. Is it $100,000, $200,000 or two million dollars? Clearly, this common idea is not a goal for it can't be measured along the way or identified when it's achieved.

An adequate definite goal would be, "I plan to save $100,000 and retire when I reach the age of sixty-five." Both conditions are identifiable and may be measured between the beginning and the ending. At age fifty-five, that person would know that he or she has only ten more years until that planned retirement age. If that person has saved $30,000, then he or she would know that the money target is about thirty percent complete. This is a definite goal.

People don't fail to reach goals because they can't reach those goals. They fail to reach goals because:

- They only dream of long-term goals
- They fail to assign clear short-term goals
- They don't assign definite and identifiable goals
- They fail to take the first step

Clearly, people who fail simply don't seem to understand the importance of adequately assigning and properly striving to reach simple goals. They tend to over-dramatize and over-complicate a simple process.

Developing a Success Attitude

Isn't it amazing how many people dream of being successful, but are defeated with a negative and grumpy attitude before they begin the success process? Before they even assign themselves a short-term goal, if they understand that process, they lament that, "It's probably not going to work, anyway." If these people have any possibility of becoming successful, it's only because they accidentally step into it—which is a rare and unusual occurrence. Ordinarily, success happens only because it's made to happen.

Developing and displaying a success attitude is one of the most important requirements to become successful. Many people are fortunate enough to have developed, naturally, a good attitude or a successful attitude in their normal life development. Others, however, have difficulty in this process, for it doesn't occur naturally— even if they desperately want to display a happy, optimistic and successful attitude.

The following steps will explain to those who want to develop a success attitude how to do it. This process is identified as the DASA (Developing a Success Attitude) plan. The DASA plan includes the following steps: start the day okay, learn to be relaxed, emulate positive people, continue self-improvement, learn to empathize and self-evaluation.

1. DASA Step One—Start the day okay

One of the major secrets to success is for a person to feel that he or she deserves, or is entitled to, success. A person who has this feeling anticipates good events and conclusions. A person who doesn't have this feeling doesn't expect good things to happen. A feeling of anticipating good things to happen allows those good things to happen and doesn't block those good and positive events.

THE SAME EVENTS USUALLY OCCUR, IT'S ONLY THE REALIZATION AND THE RESPONSE TO THOSE EVENTS THAT DETERMINE SUCCESS OR FAILURE IN ONE'S LIFE.

To start the day okay is a simple and easy process. One simply determines to begin the day positively instead of negatively or unconcerned. If one starts the day unconcerned, normal negative influences and surroundings may cause that person to develop negative tendencies during the day without realizing what's happened. One may be sure of beginning the day with a good positive feeling only by intending to begin the day with a good and positive feeling about himself or herself. A person begins the day okay by simply telling himself or herself at the beginning of each day that he or she is a good person that good things will happen to.

To establish and reinforce this positive feeling, one should routinely make a positive statement as soon as he or she awakens each morning. Each person should train himself or herself to begin each day with a positive statement that will set the tone for that day. The positive statement should be simple, straight-forward and positive. For example, a typical statement might be one of the following:

"It's another day, and I'm here to enjoy it."
"I'm sure I can improve myself today."
"Some problems might occur today, but I can handle them."
"Look out world! Here I come!"

The particular statement isn't important as long as the principle of positive reinforcement to oneself is maintained. Any positive statement will work, but it must be used consistently, everyday. (My daily reinforcement statement is, "Thanks for this first breath this morning.")

One should be alert to avoid statements that are only wishful thinking statements. A wishful thinking statement doesn't reinforce a positive outlook, and if it doesn't come true it will probably add to any negative feelings and tendencies. Wishful thinking statements are those such as:

"I certainly hope I have a good day today."
"The teacher might be better today than yesterday."
"Maybe I can avoid any problems today."

It should be easy to determine the shortcomings of these wishful thinking statements, or others similar to these. The wished for conditions rarely come true, and their failure usually results in more negative reinforcement.

The fundamental purpose for the positive statement to start one's day positively is to acknowledge that normal problems will probably occur, but the person acknowledges that condition and is prepared to deal with whatever happens. That understanding and acceptance of ability and confidence is the primary basis for developing a successful attitude.

2. DASA Step Two—Learn to be relaxed

A person cannot maximize his or her abilities and confidence in situations of apprehension and tension. To understand and develop a success attitude, one must develop a self-presence that will allow that person to concentrate on solving real problems, instead of worrying about the existence of those problems and questions. Worrying about problems has never solved any problems. Trying to avoid problems has never solved any problems. Believing that one is not capable of solving problems prevents other problems from being solved.

The correct way to solve problems and questions is to concentrate on finding solutions—not to worry about the existence of those problems. To find solutions, one must be prepared to accept problems as natural occurrences, and also be prepared to handle them, routinely. Consequently, the key to being relaxed to handle problems is to be mentally prepared for their occurrence.

One might ask, "How can a football quarterback make decisions so quickly and accurately within split-seconds while people are trying to pounce all over him?" One might also ask, "How can a matador in the bull ring remain so calm while a mad bull is trying to gore him with two giant horns." Another equally interesting question is, "How can a ballerina dance on her toes for an hour and make those motions seem effortless?"

All those questions have the same basic answer—they have planned, practiced and prepared to do what they do. Since they are prepared, they only have to do it, not worry about whether or not they can do it.

The quarterback, the matador and the ballerina should serve as examples for every person who wants to become relaxed to enhance the attitude development process. There's no secret and there's no magic to it. One simply must be prepared to do what he or she plans to do.

A typist cannot be relaxed unless that typist can type. A laborer cannot work consistently unless that laborer learns to maintain a healthy body. A grocery clerk cannot function comfortably unless that person understands numbers and words. A manager cannot manage effectively and consistently unless he or she has prepared to be a manager. In all cases, a person must train to be prepared to do whatever that person chooses to do. If not, relaxation will not be possible. If relaxation is not developed, a comfortable positive attitude remains only an illusive dream. The success process cannot be completed.

3. DASA Step Three—Emulate a positive person

Another action that one might take toward continuing to improve his or her attitude is to emulate those positive actions of a person who's respected for having a good attitude and a positive personality. Although personality, itself, is not the primary motive for trying to improve one's attitude, it's nevertheless, an outward expression of an attitude. A friendly personality usually expresses a positive attitude.

While beginning to improve one's attitude by setting clear goals and learning to be prepared, a person might not know how to express these new positive feelings and emotions. Since many people are recognized for their natural ability to exhibit friendly personalities and positive attitudes, these persons should be used as patterns to emulate, for an outward expression of attitudes.

What are some of the characteristics to observe for emulation? These would include most of the following:

- Upper body mannerisms—especially hand motions
- Facial expressions
- Voice—tone and inflection
- Diction and clarity of speech
- Timing of expressive participation
- Active listening to other speakers

Naturally, one would not perfectly try to emulate another person. The results of that effort might seem artificial. However, those positive attributes of other people may be used as guides to develop one's own attitude and personality style that's comfortable and positive for that person. Good qualities of other people, and there are many to choose from, should not be overlooked as a reference toward determining and estabishing a success attitude.

4. DASA Step Four—Read self-improvement articles

This is an easy and simple action to accomplish. One should simply read books and other developmental articles that guide one to a better personality and to better physical health. There are hundreds—maybe thousands—of books in any bookstore in the self-improvement section that may guide a person toward improvement in personality, attitude, self-confidence, getting along with other people, becoming conversationally active and any other area of concern that one might have regarding his or her attitude, personality and confidence.

Even if a person can't afford to buy books at a bookstore, that's not a good excuse to avoid this important step of self- development. Many of these good books are available in libraries, and library books are free—assuming of course that they are returned on time.

Other good sources of self-development articles are available other than in books. Magazines and newspapers also have articles that give short and simple guidance to help one improve specific areas of his or her life. Most articles in magazines and newspapers refer, in some small way, to social interaction and attitude although the article might not be designed for that specific purpose. Reading —any reading—is always a form of self-improvement. Many people make the serious mistake of avoiding reading as soon as they graduate from high school.

5. DASA Step Five—Avoid anger by empathizing

This action step might be somewhat difficult for many people, especially those who tend to want to be "right" about everything. Anger or other types of negative emotional displays tend to cause irrational and illogical perceptions and behavior. Anger and high emotions certainly don't indicate that one has started the day okay with intentions to keep it that way. Neither does anger and high emotions indicate that one has learned to relax and expect problems to occur that may be solved. Steps one and two of the DASA plan will certainly be jeopardized if one is controlled by anger or other negative emotions.

In reality, a success attitude cannot be developed by a person who's ruled by negative emotions. That condition would indicate that the person is subject to his or her environment and not in control of it.

Empathy is a positive approach to remain in control of one's destiny. Empathy simply means to consider the situation from the other person's point of view. It means to walk in the other person's shoes for awhile—to see things from his or her perspective. A person who can empathize is a person who can use rationalization to solve problems and answer questions. A person who can empathize learns to focus more on the question or the problem at hand than to focus on protecting a fragile ego or self-perceived weakness. A person who can see things and situations from different points of view from a broader perspective is a social person who may become comfortable, confident and relaxed. This person really becomes a problem-solver rather than remaining a problem-maker.

6. DASA Step Six—Analysis and reflection

This last step is probably the most important step, for it's an incorporation of all the other DASA steps. At the end of each day, every day, one should reserve time to analyze and reflect upon

actions and reactions that occurred that day, and to determine what
went well and what might have been improved to enhance the DASA
plan. Some basic and standard questions should include:

- "Did I remember to start the day okay?"
- "Was I prepared for special events today?"
- "Was I relaxed most of the day?"
- "Did I observe any actions that I should emulate?"
- "Did I perform any personal self-improvement?"
- "Did I become angry or upset? Why?"
- "Was I too ego-involved to consider other views?"
- "What do I need to improve for tomorrow?"

This reflection exercise should be performed daily until the
desired actions and steps become part of one's normal character and
personality. When this occurs, a person may then feel the burning
power of a success attitude. This attitude also gives a clearer understanding to the importance of specific goals.

A powerful success plan begins with clear goals and the right
attitude to accomplish those clear goals. Success does not just
happen, it must be made to happen. Even with a good success plan,
however, there will be powerful influences and obstacles working
against that plan. These negative influences must also be understood, for they are powerful enough to defeat even the best success
plan.

Determination

Determination is related to a person's direct focus and personal pursuit to become successful at reaching a goal. Some people
interpret this concept of getting ahead as gaining more material
possessions. Consequently, their focus may be on getting things,
rather than doing things that result in receiving more rewards for
work, study and determination.

Often, the despair and futility of trying to get ahead may
influence a person to evolve into a problem student and even a
problem worker. These problem persons may ordinarily be identified by some of the following characteristics:

- The person's performance becomes weak in quantity and
  quality
- The person's attitude becomes disruptive
- The person's actions are more controlled by a group

This misinterpretation by some people of the ideas and conditions of getting ahead is one of their major obstacles to focus and
determination. A person must remain focused and determined to

accomplish those actions that will eventually result in an evolutionary advancement to that person's life. To develop a fixation on material possessions, and to ignore those methods to achieve those possessions, will cause a person to abandon the control that he or she has, ultimately and justly, to be rewarded. That ultimate reward will include higher esteem as well as more material things.

When a person has a good success plan, he or she must prepare to begin those actions. Preparing means to train, to become skilled, and to develop a positive mental state of mind. This must be accomplished by accepting positive values that might not be part of one's normal culture.

Personal values play an important role that's not ordinarily considered as a serious success influence. Many beliefs and opinions are reflected as personal values. These values help to determine the manner in which a person acts and reacts to work and educational requirements. Those values also often determine that person's attitude toward leadership, the desire for responsibility, his or her confidence level, the degree of involvement and the eagerness to cooperate.

Students' values in the school environment aren't relevant if those values don't conflict with values of that educational environment. If a conflict in values does exist between those students and the environment, those students may become rebellious, experience absences, exhibit low morale and refuse to become or remain productive.

Sources for developing values include one's important associates and peers, authorities and hero figures, emotional situations, and media communications. Ordinarily, the values and perceptions of a person, including a student, would be the same as those of the person's socioeconomic culture. The strongest influence that helps to develop student values is family culture, family stability and family support.

Self-Improvement

Everyone is for self-improvement. No one's against it. Everyone usually agrees that self-improvement is a good thing that everybody should do.

Everybody plans to take a course in something, or train in something, to improve themselves. How many people actually follow through on their plans to take a course, or to begin a training program? Why do those good intentions to pursue one's self-improvement rarely become actual events? Why do people fail to do those important things they are frequently planning to do? Self-improvement will be analyzed to help reinforce the necessity for personal self-improvement, and to identify many reasons that prevent its occurrence. Hopefully, reinforcement to the concept of self-improvement will help a student, or any other person, find motivation within himself or herself to begin that important process with a small first step.

People need a constant flow of self-improvement for three reasons:

1. One needs a continuous flow of ideas and information for self-enlightenment. One's mind works at higher efficiency and excitement when it's learning new things that it can assimilate. The more information that one's mind has, the faster this assimilation process can occur. This is the basis for the narrow view and limited personality of people in the lower social class of society. Their lack of positive self-development has limited their ability to interpret new information, objectively.
2. There are many self-improvement methods and sources that can give a person much personal satisfaction and joy.
3. Constant self-improvement is the best and most positive way to advance one's career.

Since people understand that self-improvement is a good thing that everyone should do, why are so few people actually doing it? Why do people, including students, wait for something to happen to them without using free time to improve themselves either intellectually, mentally or professionally to make those things happen? Is there not some degree of guilt by letting that time waste away? What's the reluctance?

This reluctance is caused by barriers to self-improvement. These barriers are the real, or imagined, reasons and excuses that keep a person from taking first positive steps. These barriers are easy to identify and categorize. They include:

1. One doesn't need more self-improvement. The person's life is progressing, so why should that person do something that's unnecessary? This is the lack of incentive barrier.
2. Fear of failure at trying to do something new or different. This is the doubt barrier.
3. The dislike of being forced into a time schedule. This is the lack of freedom barrier.
4. Not having enough time to do everything. This is the too busy barrier.

5. Not having enough money to buy books or pay for classes. This is the cost barrier.
6. Not having the right courses, or the right books, available. This is the selection barrier.

Do any of these barriers sound familiar? Everyone has good reasons and excuses for not doing something. That's one of the great human traditions Many of these barriers are also real, and present real problems to people who sincerely try to improve themselves.

Avoid Frustration

A good success plan must also include the ability to solve problems and to face ordinary daily life without yielding to the temptation of becoming frustrated. Everyone's life has many bumpy roads along the way. The manner in which these bumpy roads are traveled will have a great influence over one's eventual success. Frustration is a normal reaction to many of these bumps in the road of everyday living.

Two actions may be taken to learn to face these bumpy roads without falling into the normal practice of developing frustration. These actions are simple and easy to learn.

First, one must learn to have a good positive attitude—a success attitude. Some suggestions to develop a success attitude have already been given. Once that success attitude has been developed, a person will possess a trait of self-presence. This trait will allow a person to accept problems as challenges to be solved rather than as obstacles that are barriers.

Secondly, one must learn the simple problem-solving process, since those bumps in the road of life are now problems to be solved and not insurmountable barriers. This problem-solving process has only six steps:

1. Identify the real problem—not just the symptoms
2. Understand the problem—by a full analysis
3. List several alternative solutions
4. Choose the best solution
5. Use that solution
6. Follow-up and evaluate the results

This problem-solving process might seem too simple to be a real consideration. It isn't. Many problems are never solved because: the real problem is never identified—only a symptom of a problem, people don't consider alternative solutions, and many people are afraid of failure—so they don't use any solution.

Improve Communications Skills

To become successful, a person must be able to communicate well. This is particularly true for students.

Communications include three abilities. This doesn't include the normal sending, receiving, interpreting and feedback process that's popularly discussed, although these are parts of the three abilities. The three abilities that are important here include: reading, activating communications and communicating effectively.

Reading

Reading is the basis for higher learning. A person who cannot read well simply will be handicapped in the learning process. This doesn't mean that the person will not be successful, it means that the person will not be a positively open person who will reach his or her highest level of potential. Reading is the exercise that should be given the top priority in any educational environment—including that supervised by a parent at home.

Activating Communications

Many people in society, including students, are shy, withdrawn or lack confidence (often because they can't read well.) Teachers and parents must recognize these shy symptoms and help children and students to overcome these handicaps. If a person is more actively involved in the communications process, that person will more clearly understand reasons and purposes for improving his or her communications skills.

Communicating Effectively

To communicate with purpose, authority and credibility, a person must be able to communicate effectively. This means that a person must be able to make himself or herself clearly understood, that the communications must be appropriate, and that the grammar in the communications must be adequate to give the speaker a certain level of credibility.

Communications skills are so important in the general success process that they shouldn't be ignored or disregarded at any level of a person's career. Although the proper places to begin developing these skills are in school and at home, this development must continue throughout one's career.

Improving Interpersonal Relationships

Success must eventually involve other people. It would probably be rare, indeed, if a person could become successful in a social vacuum. Other people, and other people's ideas, are important to one's success. For example, in a school environment, the relationship between a teacher and a student directly affects the happiness and the objectivity of that student.

Many books and other articles are available in bookstores and libraries to help one improve his or her interpersonal relationship skills; therefore, a long statement will not be made redundantly, here. Three concepts are so important, however, that they must be presented as guiding reminders:

1. Make the other person feel important. Avoid the word "I" as much as possible.
2. There are no definites in life. Everything does not always have a right and wrong or a true or false. Therefore, a person doesn't have to win all the arguments.
3. Courtesy is the oil to success. It reduces life's friction.

These success-planning concepts, alone, will not assure that a person, a student, will be successful. There are many other obstacles and barriers that routinely work against one's success plans. One thing is certain, however. That is, that without a success plan to become successful, one probably has a definite plan to fail.

How can this success plan be used? It's unlikely that young students will understand the concepts of this plan by themselves by just reading these words. Parents and teachers are encouraged to formulate these basic concepts within their own frameworks of reference, and to use these concepts consistently and routinely at the best times when their students or children are most receptive.

Furthermore, a class on success-planning and personal development should be developed for each school. This would reinforce the concept that success is not something that just happens to a person—it's something that a person can plan to do for himself or herself.

General Skills

In addition to teaching students how to learn, how to develop good communications skills and how to develop a success plan, schools should also teach students basic and fundamental work skills. These fundamental work skills would not include those specialized skills ordinarily developed in vocational or job training programs. A brief analysis of the weakness and inefficiency of secondary vocational training programs, however, might be appropriate to define these different concepts.

High school vocational programs were envisioned and planned to fulfill a desperate need in high schools. That idealistic goal was to provide students with the opportunity to plan and train for a career instead of advancing into higher education, for those students who wanted to begin a career. An alternate goal was to prepare students who might later leave the education system with a practical career to permit them to be employable. Vocational training has had some positive effect; however, it's never reached a significant level of influence within the education system. There are four reasons for this lack of greater effectiveness:[11]

1. Vocational programs are associated with weak students
2. It's considered valuable, but "not for my child"
3. Vocational facilities and equipment are costly
4. Some tenured teachers teach non-applicable skills

In summary, vocational training hasn't fulfilled its needed role in the education system due to emphasis and cost. Although it's recognized as a necessary approach, and a valuable alternative, it has a negative stigma. It's ordinarily considered as an alternative class for students who aren't smart enough to do well in school. Furthermore, educators, counselors and parents encourage students to plan for advanced education upon graduation from high school. Society, including educators and parents, suggests that anything less than that implies failure.

The other reason that vocational training hasn't been extensively used is the high cost. Costs of establishing vocational centers that would train for multiple careers, in every school, would be prohibitive.

General workplace skills training, however, would be a more realistic alternative. It would also probably be a more acceptable alternative to parents who want to keep their children from the pits of vocational training. General workplace skills would include those universal skills that may be used in various work environments regardless of the specific details of that occupation. These could be conducted in most average classrooms—without high costs.

Some examples include:

- Workplace requirements, concepts and terminology
- Typing and keyboard skills (typewriter or computer)
- Office administration (filing and organizing)

- Office equipment operation
- Telephone etiquette
- Customer service relations
- Warehousing concepts and practices
- Distribution and shipping techniques
- Occupational safety
- Security of company assets

These are some major examples of general workplace skills and requirements that are applicable to many jobs, but not to one specific occupation.

This training would prepare students to enter most jobs lacking only the technical training of those specific jobs. MOST WORKERS WHO FAIL AT THEIR JOBS DON'T FAIL FROM THEIR LACK OF TECHNICAL SKILLS. Those who fail, or who become problem workers, do so from their lack of interest, motivation, general job skills or work ethic. These general job skills would apply to students whether they begin a career as a dropout, as a high school graduate or after higher education.

Summary

This approach toward an enhanced education process requires no new education philosophies or ideologies. It may fit comfortably within the current system that, in itself, serves an honorable and high purpose. Most training and techniques that now exist in the education process are aimed toward directly improving student's knowledge. Nothing substantial could be accomplished without that basic knowledge that schools provide.

The ideas offered in this chapter are to complement that knowledge so that it may be used more efficiently. These suggestions are not intended to replace current practices.

These ideas to improve communications effectiveness, learning skills, success planning and general skills are offered to make the current education system really do what it desperately tries to do— to produce students who can contribute to their own welfare and to the welfare of society. Fifty to seventy percent of our students do that now, partially as a result of the current education system. Many of those have innate abilities that would allow them to become successful regardless of the education process.

There are the other thirty to fifty percent of our students, however, who fail to be motivated, inspired, trained or educated to a level that will force them into the mainstream of our productive economic society. These students are "the education dilemma" and are the objects of the ideas and suggestions in this chapter.

Part Three, which follows, gives more specific and detailed guidance to those students and their parents to help them become part of the contributing economic process of our country. Although society and the education system can help a student become successful, the major determinants to that student's success is within himself or herself, the family and the influencing culture. The formal education, itself, plays only a minor role in the success of a child.

A student reared in a family culture that anticipates, supports and is accustomed to success will most likely become successful. On the other hand, a student reared in a family culture that has no history of success or that doesn't understand the value of aspirations and effort will most likely not achieve a high level of personal success.

CHAPTER SEVEN

PROBLEM STUDENTS

The question of how to manage problem students within the education system is so dominant that it needs special attention. Problem students not only disrupt the education process, statistics also show that many of our social problems result from our inability to train many of those students toward acceptable social behavior. Many problem students drop out of school, many of those who drop out of school begin criminal activities, and many of those who become criminals are placed in prisons at a high monetary and economic cost to society.

Before we can make sense from an analysis of behavioral correction, it's probably helpful to understand some fundamental basis for the cause of that problem behavior. An excellent source of that understanding is provided by Bertrand Russell, an educator, philosopher and mathematician who wrote and taught in the early 1900s. Russell wrote:[12]

> "The most distinctive feature by which the evolutionary status of these (our) early ancestors is fixed is the size of the brain, which increased fairly rapidly until it reached its present capacity, but has now been stationary for hundreds of thousands of years. During these hundreds of thousands of years Man has improved in knowledge, in acquired skill and in social organization, but not, so far as can be judged, in congenital intellectual capacity.
> —One of the things that cause stress and strain in human social life is that it is possible, up to a point, to become aware of rational grounds for a behavior not prompted by natural instinct. But when such behavior strains natural instinct too severely nature takes her revenge by producing either listlessness or destructiveness, either of which may cause a structure inspired by reason to break down."

Bertrand Russell's ideas are related to those ideas later expressed by Berelson and Steiner.(9) Berelson and Steiner suggested that the lower cultures in society are characterized by a narrow personality range. Their identification of a narrow personality is basically the same condition that could be described as a lower intellectual capacity expressed by Russell. Intellectual capacity must be described as the ability to reason and negotiate ideas outside the confines of basic instincts. Perhaps those basic, and primitive, instincts that Bertrand Russell mentioned are the same as the narrow personality that Berelson and Steiner identify.

To develop a correction process for problem students, or other children, that process must be based on a fundamental cause of those problems. Until another fundamental cause might be determined there's no other alternative to the fundamental idea that the correction process must be designed to alter those primitive instincts and those narrow personalities; and to replace those instincts with a higher intellectual capacity for those problem students to conceptualize and rationalize.

Problem students must be taught a broader personality to accept and to cooperate with the normal expectations of society. The purpose for this chapter is to assist in that goal.

Problem students will be described and discussed by two categories, or dimensions, of problems. First will be the dropout student, or the potential dropout student. These are generally labeled as "at risk" students, for they are at risk of failure and despair or of dropping out of school. Secondly will be the active problem student. This includes the student who's disruptive, uncooperative and exhibits a strong tendency toward antisocial behavior.

At Risk Students

These students aren't necessarily the social misfits or the disruptive students who cause negative distractions in a classroom. At risk students may simply be students who lack the same level of academic skills that more advantaged students have, or those who lack the cultural background to support good academic efforts. If these students eventually drop out of school some will be somewhat successful, some will be a financial and moral burden to society, and others will likely tend to become social misfits or even serious criminals. In either case, most high school dropouts will not contribute positively to society, or to themselves.

Efforts must be made to raise the aspirations of these at risk students to allow them to find success for themselves in the normal school environment. Most of the information in this book is aimed at converting these students from despair and futility toward higher aspirations and normal expectations of personal success. The effectiveness of the education process will be determined by the success of this goal—not by improving the grades of students who will be successful, regardless of the type of education system. That thirty percent of students, approximately, must be reached to keep them in school and to help them feel successful.

To keep them in school it's important to understand why they choose to drop out of school. Some of those reasons will be discussed next. It should also be remembered that these reasons exist primarily within the narrow personality of the lower social cultures. Students from higher cultures, although they might suffer from some of the same negative tendencies, ordinarily manage to understand the consequences of yielding to those temptations to quit. Educators must help at risk students overcome these negative motivations, along with the enhanced curriculum explained in the previous chapter, to bring these students into the normal education process.

Tired of School

One often used reason for a student to quit school is that he or she just got "tired" of school. It wasn't fun, it was boring and the student wanted to do something different. A person who would use this reason obviously doesn't understand the purpose or the reason for going to school. School is not necessarily fun and exciting unless one wants to make it fun and exciting. The purpose for school is to learn about life so that one can learn to make it fun and exciting. Life is not intrinsically anything. One's perception of life and one's participation in it are the things that determine what life is to that person. If one expects life to be fun and exciting by just observing it, he or she will certainly be surprised. Life is nothing more than a mirror. One gets back no more than he or she puts into it.

Needs a Job

Another reason for dropping out of school is to get a job to make money. In most cases, this is nothing more than fantasy and wishful thinking. The only jobs that one will find, before graduating from high school, are those jobs that no one needs or wants. These are usually the very lowest level jobs that create weariness, hopelessness and despair without enough pay to even pay house rent. These are the jobs that usually trap a person into permanent, long-term forced labor. These are the jobs that will embarrass a person two or three years later, when that person compares career status with high school peers who continued their education. Except in very rare cases, a student traps himself or herself into being a permanent dependent of his or her family or the state.

Stress and Embarrassment

Sometimes students quit school to avoid situations that are stressful or embarrassing. That stress or embarrassment could be caused by any problem faced by students. This might include any of the following:

- A general feeling of alienation
- A lack of peer friendships in school
- Believing that teachers dislike them
- The embarrassment of low grades and scores
- Stress and embarrassment of being poor
- Inability to own "expected" clothing
- Reputation or actions of a family member
- Despair and lack of aspirations
- The fear of being unattractive
- Pregnancy

Students must be taught, in a normal classroom environment where different social groups and cultures may interact to offer peer reinforcement, that to drop out of school, to quit, for any reason is a serious mistake. They must be taught that to drop out, especially for reasons of stress or embarrassment, makes one a "quitter," one who refuses to face normal challenges.

They must also be taught that if pressure and embarrassment are used as reasons to quit school, then it will be difficult for those who quit to achieve any success in life, for they will have set the pattern to use those excuses as reasons to fail at other things. They must learn to understand that an average person will always face at least some pressure and embarrassment in the normal process of living. If a student chooses to drop out of school, that student must face even greater pressures and embarrassments in the future that will be more difficult to overcome.

The Too-Smart Student

Then, of course, there's the student who's so smart that he or she thinks school is a complete waste of time. Since this student already knows everything, there's really no need to learn more about mathematics, algebra, grammar, geography, history, economics, finance, biology, chemistry, sociology or health. According to this student, these subjects are a waste of time because there will never be any need to refer to or use this information.

Isn't it amazing how much these people forget when they start competing for jobs? They forget how to fit in and they forget how to find their places in life. Usually, they go from job to job because employers and supervisors cannot tolerate the superiority that these persons try to exhibit. Traditionally, they have an attitude problem. Unfortunately, these persons rarely learn to find a comfortable place in life because they are too busy trying to justify themselves to themselves.

The Lazy Student

Finally, there's the student who's just "plain lazy." Robert Schuller counsels, "The temptation to laziness never grows old."[13] These students are ordinarily good easy-going people who don't have, or cannot find, the motivation to care or to study. They tend to fade away and disappear. Once they leave school, they are never heard from again, at least until they become challenged by their self-image, or unless they become burdens of society.

Summary—At Risk Students

The education system, schools, must teach students that although reasons that tempt one to drop out of school are personally important at that time, they aren't nearly as serious as the result of dropping out of school. They must be helped to understand that they discredit themselves and their families, they disappoint their friends, and they actively choose to be less than they can be. And, they will most likely contribute to the economic problems of our society.

Their action of dropping out certainly indicates they have no concern for other people and events around them. They are selfishly concerned only about their feelings and their own undeveloped self-interests. To drop out of school suggests they have not been mature enough to consider the probable results of their decisions and actions. Perhaps these reasons and excuses for students who choose to drop out of school should be included in the success planning course, under the title of social responsibility.

Problem Students

Problem students, defined here, include those students who lack acceptable discipline or studentship skills. These are not necessarily the lazy student, the uninspired student and the slow student. The problem student is the student who disrupts the education process by exhibiting unacceptable behavior in the school environment, particularly in the classroom. Problem students are typified by the following examples:

- They routinely refuse to do their homework
- They refuse to take tests seriously
- They disrupt any class group assignment
- They try to be the center of attention
- They try to intimidate their schoolmates
- They harass younger students
- They are routinely uncooperative
- They disregard teachers' instructions
- They are unpleasant to be around
- They participate in more serious antisocial behavior

A problem student is one who doesn't allow teachers to enjoy their role as teachers, which should be one of society's most enjoyable vocations. Allowing a problem student to remain in a classroom is unfair to that teacher. Furthermore, a problem student doesn't allow other students to gain the most from the education process. That's unfair to those students. Basically, problem students create tragedy for the education process. They must be positively controlled or quickly removed from that normal environment to permit the education process to work.

Now, the question becomes, "What should be done with those problem students?" Traditionally, that problem has been forced upon teachers, counselors and other administrators in the school system. The wrong people have been tasked with maintaining that extraordinary disciplinary requirement. THAT FUNCTION SHOULD NOT BE FORCED UPON TEACHERS AND SCHOOL ADMINISTRATORS. A teacher's role should be to teach in an environment that will allow that teacher to focus on teaching. A teacher should not be required to be a full-time disciplinarian or baby-sitter for antisocial students. Others should be tasked with that responsibility. They include parents and specialized campus trainers. These concepts will be analyzed next.

The Parent's Responsibility

Parents are solely responsible for preparing their children to comply with social norms and disciplinary expectations when they send their children to a school to be taught those things that schools are chartered to teach. Discipline is often a by-product of the education process, but it's not a direct task of the normal education process. Society doesn't expect that to be done in the classroom. Society expects that to be done in the home. Since parents are in charge of the home environment—or should be—then parents are in charge of their children's discipline.

Unfortunately, too many parents either don't or can't fulfill that basic responsibility. Many of those parents apparently assume that schools can correct any disciplinary problem that their children might have, so they don't have to worry about it. Other parents seem to think that once their child is out of sight, then the child is no longer their responsibility. Other parents often claim that the school environment is the cause of their child's disciplinary problem—since teachers don't know how to treat them. There are also other parents who sincerely try to teach their children proper discipline and behavior but fail. That failure is usually blamed on the parent. We shouldn't ignore the possibility, however, that some children are too instinctively antisocial to be disciplined by a normal parent without professional help.

Regardless of the rationalization and the complications, parents are still the source of discipline and acceptable social behavior of their children. This responsibility should not be shifted from parents—and this responsibility should not be accepted by the normal school system. Parents should be assisted in this process, however, when the task is too great for a parent to handle alone. The first step should always begin with the parent.

The first active step in the disciplinary process should be parental visibility in the classroom. This should vary by degrees. As a routine practice, parents should be invited to visit the classroom of their child at any time. They should know all the other teachers of that same grade level, as well as the names of teachers in the grade at one higher level. They should also be encouraged to visit at least quarterly.

At the onset of a disciplinary problem with a child, the parent of that child should be asked to be present in the classroom until the child corrects his or her behavior. If the disciplinary problem becomes severe, the parent should be lawfully required to be present to enforce proper discipline of that child. Of course this might cause hardship for those parents who work at the same time their children are in school. Although this may be a hardship, the success of the education process is too important to the survival of our economy - and maybe even our country—to allow anyone to avoid his or her personal responsibility. If the parent cannot maintain discipline of his or her child in the classroom, the second level of discipline should apply.

Alternative Schools

The second level of control should be alternative school.

Alternative schools should be based on two principles. First, the school should be designed to allow more concentrated training on the social and disciplinary skills. The success planning curriculum described earlier would directly apply to this school. Secondly, the regular school system should be protected from deterioration by quickly removing these students who tend to create that deterioration. Parents' active participation should be required in those alternative school programs.

Many alternative schools now exist in many school districts. Some are successful and some are not. Perhaps more attention to the social skills, an enhanced success planning curriculum and active participation by parents would make more of those schools even more successful.

By applying the Pareto Principle, it could reasonably be estimated that approximately one of every five students who attended an alternative school would need a higher level of training to learn, to begin to learn or to comply with social norms. The Pareto Principle was conceptualized by Vilfredo Pareto, a statistician, who determined that most abnormal deviations (80 percent) are caused by only a small number of events (20 percent.) This is often called the 80/20 rule.[14]

These are also the same students who are at higher risk to begin criminal activity if they aren't assimilated into normal social expectations and aspirations. One statistic confirms that Pareto's Principle is, in fact, valid. Approximately twenty percent of young black males in our society are in jail or prison, or have been, for criminal activity.

Another level must be established to help assimilate these students who cannot be reached in standard alternative schools. That level will be described next.

Campus Training

If standard statistics and deviations can be accepted as probability, then it's probable that society should plan to train twenty percent of those students who begin an alternative school program in a more structured environment. The standard alternative program will not reach those students. This more highly structured training environment would include a residential on-campus training program.

The idea of a residential program is not new to education concepts. A residential training program was recommended in the

Third Report, July, 1970, by the National Advisory Council on Vocational Education to the Commissioner of Education at that time.[11] That report states:

> "There is mounting evidence that America must make an investment in residential schools for some adolescents who cannot cope with their homes or neighborhoods. A nation whose boarding schools are conducted only for the wealthy and for those under juvenile court sentence has misplaced its priorities. There are young people who will respond to remedial education and career preparation only if separated from home and neighborhood conditions which make it impossible for them to learn in a day-school setting."

Although the focus of that report was aimed toward career education, the same idea should be even more applicable to social integration. That report has been ignored since it was submitted in 1970. Could the implementation of that idea, at that time, have significantly reduced many of the social integration problems that we have today?

From a practical point, the program recommended in that report was unrealistic. It recommended a residential school in "every major metropolitan community and every poor rural area."

It would be unrealistic to expect that school budgets could fund that idea, universally. It's not unrealistic, however, to plan and budget regional residential schools that would accommodate that twenty percent who couldn't be assimilated within basic alternative schools. Those alternative schools are now, and would be, located in more centrally located areas—perhaps within or adjacent to regular schools. The number of students to house could be determined by estimating from that twenty percent of students in alternative schools.

What should be the concept of operations for residential schools? The following ideas could be considered:

- The environment should be that of cadet training
- A standard curriculum should be taught
- Self-reliance and confidence should be instilled
- A strong physical exercise program should be used
- Operant conditioning (Skinner) should be used - rewards
- People from disciplined vocations should participate (Firefighters, police, military)
- New students should be guided by "upper classmen"
- When trained, students should be allowed to remain in that school if space is available. Otherwise they should return to their regular school.

Now, one might suggest that a residential program is too expensive to build and to operate. One might also suggest that it's not morally or socially correct to separate, involuntarily, a child into a specialized environment. Those who make these suggestions are probably correct from the perception of individual rights.

On the other hand, society must be protected to perpetuate itself to maintain the opportunity for individual rights. Wanton disregard for the safety of society is prelude to a hazardous future. Individual rights must be accompanied by individual responsibility and expectations. If those individual responsibilities and expectations don't support those rights, then the access to those rights must be adjusted. Students should not be left to their own devices to become burdens to society. This is unfair and immoral to those students, and it's unfair and immoral for society.

There's also the consideration of cost. This will be answered by stating one fact, and asking two simple questions. The fact—it costs at least $35,000 to $45,000 to keep one prisoner incarcerated each year, year after year. The questions: (1) How much would it cost to house and educate one student for one year? $5000 to $10,000? (2) To save money, can we afford not to have a special residential training program?

Summary

Problem students are problems to themselves and to society.

Many of those problem students are also problems to their families who might make sincere efforts to train their children to conform to expectations and norms of society.

There are two types of problem students. One is the student who simply lacks average ability or who refuses to develop his or her potential. These students aren't necessarily direct problems to society, but their lack of ability or motivation to contribute positively to society might result in their becoming a burden to society in the form of welfare support. With understanding and enthusiastic family support and an effective school curriculum these students may easily be trained toward success.

The other type of problem student is the true problem student. This student actively disrupts the classroom, fellow students and the education process. These students cannot be allowed to remain in the normal education system to perpetuate the ineffectiveness of education. They must quickly be removed from that purposeful environment to permit teachers to teach and real students to learn. That removal, however, should be by a process that uses only minimum emphasis and resources to correct that student's behavior.

This removal should be by graduated levels to insure that students who need only minimum guidance toward acceptable social standards receive only that minimum force. The most stringent measures should be used for only the most antisocial and disruptive students who display the most primitive and destructive behavior. Regardless of the measures used, they must be led toward productive tendencies and expectations before their primitive natures destroy themselves and become a permanent burden to society.

Yes, some of these measures might be harsh. We have no choice, however, for something must be done; and it must be done aggressively and dynamically. A biological cancer in a human's body, once it's detected, is not allowed to continue to grow—with the anticipation that it might deteriorate by itself. Something is done to remove that cancer. It's a sorry state of affairs for our country, or any country, that will allow the social cancer of antisocial behavior and crime to continue to wreak havoc without taking some action to remove that cancer. Wishing and hoping that it will disappear will not cure that problem. That problem must be cured by direct actions.

Part Three, which follows, gives more specific and detailed guidance to those students and their parents to help them become part of the contributing economic process of our country. Although society and the education system can help a student become successful, the major determinants to that student's success is within himself or herself, the family and the influencing culture. The formal eduction itself plays only a minor role in the success of a child.

A student reared in a family structure that anticipates, supports and is accustomed to success will most likely become successful. On the other hand, a student reared in a family culture that has no history of success or that doesn't understand the value of aspirations and effort will most likely not achieve a high level of personal success.

PART THREE

STUDENT
AND
PARENT
RESPONSIBILITIES
TO
DEVELOP
SUCCESSFUL
STUDENTS

CHAPTER EIGHT

PERSONAL SUCCESS PLANNING

The analysis in the first two parts of this book covered those things that contribute to an education environment and to the basic education system. An increased awareness of the education dilemma by society might have a more positive effect on that environment. Readjustment of education emphasis in the classroom to focus more on confidence and self-image for students might also provide more directly relevant guidance to help students. The most important part of education, however, that determines the success of education for each individual is each individual student's aspirations. Those aspirations are determined primarily by the individual character of a student that's formed in his or her home and cultural environment.

The highest level of social or governmental support cannot create a successful student. It can only create conditions that will allow a student to become successful. The greatest education system with the highest ideas and the best teachers cannot create a successful student. It can only give information and guidance to help that student become successful. Only the student who has at least a minimum level of intelligence and who's not handicapped by negative cultural values can create a successful student. A successful student is ultimately determined by the student and that student's parents.

The first two parts of this book analyzed things outside the control of the student and the student's parents that contribute somewhat toward creating an atmosphere that will allow a student to become successful. These things, social involvement and the

·education system, may affect the quality of education but they don't determine the quality of education for individual students. Part Three is targeted directly toward each student and his or her parents to assist them in learning how to use the education system. Even if the education system is not perfect—and it may be impossible to achieve that status—any student can learn to be successful if he or she chooses to be successful, and learns the success process.

Although the current education system is not designed for efficient results, it is nevertheless the system that a student must consider as the basis to design a personal success plan. To become successful, the inner person is more important and influential than external conditions. A student must consider the school system as merely another of those external considerations, and continue to plan for personal success.

Student Responsibilities for Success

Students must respond positively to their education challenges. They should meet those challenges and prepare themselves. In the meantime, they should put equal pressure back onto those who make economic improvement of society their responsibility. Students should let those persons know that when they have developed themselves into bright stars, that they expect to have places to shine. They should take advantage of everything they can that the education system offers, and then demand even more to challenge their abilities.

It's the responsibility of the current generation to make those places ready when students have diligently prepared themselves. The current generation has failed to do that to offer clear and valid reasons to motivate students to be successful.

How can students do this? They can do this by accomplishing two tasks. First, by becoming active and positive students. Secondly, by asking questions and writing letters, by becoming proactive in their education process. The information to help develop oneself into a good proactive student will be analyzed first.

Beginning at the Beginning

There are two phases of the education process that were introduced in Part Two. These two phases were introduced as responsibilities of the education system; however, they must be understood by parents and students to make those principles work. One is the learning phase and the other is the learning to learn phase.

The learning phase is traditionally the phase that receives all the education emphasis. This phase includes the typical teaching, listening, studying and testing functions. Parents and students cannot directly participate in the normal classroom teaching process, but as part of society they should have some influence on that process and the results of that process. Parents and students, however, are responsible for the child's participation in the other parts of that process. The student must actively listen, study and be prepared for tests and evaluations.

The other learning phase is a learning to learn phase. This phase is rarely considered or emphasized early in the education process. The learning to learn functions, when available, are presented as a business or entrepreneurial venture by organizations outside the normal school system. Since these are private profit-making ventures that must be paid by parents and students, many students are excluded from these opportunities. Many students and their families are not even aware that these opportunities exist.

Most school and education systems are totally focused on training students to memorize information to pass standardized tests. These tests may be diabolically designed to evaluate teacher performance rather than to evaluate a student's learning skills. If the goal of a school is to train students to pass a standardized test then the school cannot be focused on real student development. The focus in the early years should be on learning how to learn more easily and quickly. If not, many students will continue to be handicapped by a "blindfold of conspiracy" in the education process.

Learning to Learn—The Home

There are three basics to the learning to learn process. These can be performed only by the student, usually with encouragement, support, direction and maybe even a little extra discipline provided by the parent. Traditionally, the mother fills this role.[1] These three basics include:

Personal Success Planning

One of these basics is success planning. Success planning is explained in detail in Chapter Six, therefore that information will not be repeated here. For a brief reminder, however, success planning includes the following activities:

1. Understanding goals
2. Developing a successful attitude
3. Avoiding demotivation—determination
4. Self-development

5. Avoiding frustration
6. Improving communications skills
7. Improving interpersonal relationships

Although success planning should be part of the school curriculum this doesn't suggest that parents and students shouldn't be concerned. Teachers are responsible for providing and reinforcing information, they are not responsible for the learning process, the doing process or the discipline to do process.

Plain Old Reading

Although the subjects of mathematics and science are important to technical advancement, there's one subject that overshadows all others in the learning to learn process. That's the subject, or discipline, of "plain old reading."

Reading is essential to education and knowledge. Although audio and video cassettes are available, there aren't enough of those to create a freckle in the vast store of written information. It's essential that students learn to read well if they want to do those things that will fulfill their dreams. Students must master the art of effective reading. If not, education will not work for them for an education really only begins after a person leaves a protected school environment. If a student cannot read well, his or her education ends there.

Basic Study Skills

The third basic requirement for learning to learn is effective study skills. Without effective study skills, a student will be handicapped in the normal learning process.

Learning is relatively easy for an average person. That's assuming of course that the person understands how to learn. Learning to learn requires study skills, most of which are never included in the normal primary school or high school curriculum. The standard education procedure is that teachers teach and students should learn. Students ordinarily are not taught the skills to learn what teachers have the skills to teach. If education were a game, it would be a one-sided situation with teachers having the obvious advantage.

To become a teacher, one must know his his or her subject matter. A teacher must also learn how to teach. Both these requirements are given equal emphasis during a person's training to become a teacher.

For the typical student, in primary school or high school, dual functions are not taught. A student is expected to learn without being first trained in the techniques of learning. Some of these major learning techniques will be described here to help students become more proactive students, more successful students and more successful persons. This information is also aimed toward helping teachers and parents guide students toward effective study skills to eliminate much of the frustration and fear of learning. These study skills include:

1. Determine a study location
2. Determine a study time
3. Learn speed reading
4. Learn to read efficiently
5. Improve memory—learn to remember
6. Learn testmanship

Each of these study skills will be analyzed individually.

Study skill #1—Determine a Study Location

The first study skill is very simple, but often ignored.

It's simply to determine the best location for routine study. In the average home choices are usually limited to the living room, the kitchen table, a bedroom, or the den. Many homes don't have a den or family room.

This study location should be one that's routinely quiet, such as a bedroom, if a quiet den or study is not available. Trying to create a quiet study area in a routinely noisy area, such as at a kitchen table, is less desirable. In a routinely noisy area, the noise will be anticipated even though it might not be present as an actual distraction. Distractions, real or anticipated, are magnified for a child for they are people who are overly curious. They are also people who don't want to miss any important event.

One caution about quietness is necessary, however. The study area should not be so quiet that the child feels isolated or cut off from other people. A feeling of involvement is essential for a child even if the child must be exposed to some noise while studying.

Where is the best location to develop good study habits? The library.

Study skill #2—Determine a Routine Study Time

How often do children arrive home from school and announce, "I don't have any homework, today?" Or, how often do they say, "I finished my homework at school?" Even worse, how often do they forget to do their homework?

A daily study time, at home, should be established by parents and students, regardless of the amount of homework. This creates a proactive approach to learning. It also indicates an acceptance by students and parents that the student's learning should not be determined only by the effectiveness and performance of a teacher. It must be recognized that a teacher can only guide a student. A teacher cannot learn for a student. That actual learning process must be an activity that's shared between parents and students. The teacher merely guides the activity and evaluates the results.

Some parents might feel educationally unqualified to help their children learn. Some parents might have stressful and tiring jobs that don't allow them the luxury of time and energy to help their children learn. These parents, although unable to teach facts and formulas, can still provide their children with the most important learning basics—time, encouragement and support. Students from these families are usually those students who need more assistance and encouragement in the learning process.

Parents and students should mutually determine a standard time for study. If more time is required to complete homework, naturally that time requirement should prevail. If the student has no homework, then the student should use that time progressively for review, research or improving reading skills. Some guidelines should apply for determining that study time:

1. The standard study time should not be interpreted by the child as a form of punishment. Initial discussion for establishing a study time should be avoided during times of frustration or stress between the parent and the child. The parent should discuss the concept at a time when the relationship is harmonious, and when grades are not the dominant topic. The atmosphere should be harmonious and focused on success; not tense, and focused on bad grades.

2. The student should not be expected, or required, to study continuously throughout the study period. Concentrated study time should be approximately fifteen to twenty minutes with five to ten minute intervals. For example, a one-hour study period would result in approximately forty-five minutes of actual study time. This schedule prevents aimless reading and drowsiness, satisfies the student's curiosity of events, and results in effective study.

3. The student should not be isolated. If the student feels more comfortable and worldly with music, kept within a tolerable decibel range, then background music should be permitted during that time. The purpose for this period is to encourage a learning process—not to demonstrate parental autocratic rule. As the student begins to develop self-esteem through improved grades, that self-esteem will eventually become more important than the need to feel part of the music world, or more important than the feeling of being isolated without sounds or a person's voice.

4. Parents must constantly show interest and concern in a child's study time. This may be done by asking either specific questions or general questions. For example, a specific question would be, "What was the result on the test that you prepared for last week?" A general question would be, "Have you read anything interesting, lately?" If the child expresses strong interest in an article, the parent should ask to read that article, or material. This produces positive reinforcement for that student, and allows that student to feel important.

Study skill #3—Learn Speed Reading

Reading is the basis of most learning. If not, a person is not learning enough. This is as equally important outside school as it is during normal school activities. Most learning, after graduation, is by reading and self-development. After graduation, however, learning may be done at one's own self-determined speed. During the school years, learning is at a more controlled and a more rapid rate. Much of the learning time during school years is consumed in the function of merely reading.

Robert Zorn indicates[15], "Very few people make full use of the abilities they have as far as reading is concerned. Figures from research indicate that we use only fifteen percent of our available mental resource when we are engaged in recognizing symbols." People use only fifteen percent of their reading potential when reading. Using only fifty percent of one's potential, a person could triple his or her reading speed, with at least the same information retention.

Wouldn't it be greatly beneficial to the education process for students to triple their reading speed? A reading assignment that normally takes an hour would take only twenty minutes. A reading assignment that ordinarily takes three hours would require only one hour. That would allow extra time to study other lessons, or to concentrate more time toward a difficult subject.

Reading comprehension may also be improved by using speed reading techniques. Robert Zorn adds, "Comprehension doesn't have to be mysterious. It can be improved if you go about it properly."

Speed reading is another of those tools to help students learn how to learn. Not only does it increase a student's time for study, it also results in increased comprehension and retention, if proper concentration is given. Proper concentration is easier while speed reading, for the reader's mind doesn't have time to wander aimlessly to think about other things. If the purpose for school is to learn, why are students not taught the speed reading techniques—so they really can learn?

Study skill #4—Reading Efficiently

In his book, *Read it Right and Remember What You Read,*[16] Samuel Smith states, "Printed words are only marks on paper until some thoughtful reader gives them meaning. To communicate in language, people must agree on the ideas which their words signify."

Merely reading, and reading for meaning, are two different concepts. Merely reading is an action of letting one's eyes see words and one's brain understand those words, based upon that person's perceptions. Reading for meaning includes an analysis of the writer's ideas that are expressed by those words.

Reading for meaning requires a higher level of concentration and an inquisitive mind. It also requires specific techniques. Throughout most writing, highlighted clues are given to alert the reader to the purpose of the paragraph or the chapter. These clues are in the forms of topic sentences and summaries. For more understandable and more efficient reading, a student must learn to identify, easily, those topic sentences and summaries. In most cases, these are the main points of the writing. Other information is included as repetition, justification, explanation or rationalization for those main points.

As a training practice, students should learn to hi-lite, underline or outline key points in material they read. Marking or hi-liting is prohibited for some books; however, a good outline on separate paper is probably even better, for it's more condensed for quick review. They should also practice scanning through reading material to understand important points and ideas before they begin detailed reading of that material.

Students must be encouraged to learn a systematic approach to reading. It will make their time devoted to reading more efficient and productive for themselves, as well as for the overall education system that claims to seek ways to improve the education process.

Study skill #5—Improving the Memory Process

Many people, students, don't perform well on tests or evaluations for they simply don't remember the appropriate answers to questions—although they might know the information. They may inherently know the answers, but under stressful or different situations their minds will not let them see those answers. How many times have students remembered test answers, that they couldn't remember during test time, as soon as they walked out the door of the test room? Have these students not learned, or have they simply not remembered? Since a student is evaluated on his or her memory, not necessarily on learning, it must be concluded that learning, in test situations, is an act of remembering.

If memory, remembering, is so vital to the learning process then students must learn how to remember. This training is essential to help them become as successful as the education system claims as its purpose.

Can memory be a school subject that's taught in a classroom?

James Weinland, in *How to Improve Your Memory*[17] writes, "One can improve any ability up to the limits of his potential, or capacity. Remembering is a skill like talking, singing, dancing, reading, thinking. Everyone—unless he has some incapacitating defect—can do all these things, but with effort and training he can learn to do any or all, of them far better."

Obviously memory can be improved for any person, up to the limit of that person's ability to learn. People have different abilities and different maximum potential. If memory is so important to learning, and, if memory is so vital to grading systems; should memory not be taught in lower levels of school so that students may really use their education and success potential?

Study skill #6—Testmanship

Ultimately, the effectiveness of school systems and the efficiency of students are determined, practically, from grades or evaluations that result from tests. Tests are eventually the deciding factors. Scores from tests are plain and irrefutable labels that suggest the character and success of large school systems, small school systems and each individual student within all school systems. Even with the critical emphasis on tests and test scores school systems don't have formal classes or instruction on "testmanship."

In his book, *Testmanship*,[18] J.N. Hook explains, "Testmanship also involves skill. The best test-takers display their abilities and knowledge to advantage. Their intelligence may be only average, and so may their ability to remember. But they are test-wise; they can achieve average success on exams with only a fair amount of information."

There's a definite skill that can be learned by students to help them make better scores on tests. For example, one of those techniques is simply to understand the purpose for the test. Understanding the purpose for a test gives many clues to the answers on multiple choice and true-false tests. That little advantage could make the difference between passing and failing that test.

Schools should teach students this skill for two fundamental reasons. First, if it's an important basic skill required through life —it should be taught. If it should be taught, that's the purpose for schools—or is it? Secondly, if a student feels more comfortable with the process of taking a test, there's less stress on that student to restrict the actual learning and memory process.

Summary—Learning to Learn

To learn, students must understand how to learn. Some students learn these learning skills by random chance, by experimentation, or with the luck of being born into a family that has a history of training in these learning skills. Other students are, by chance, born into families that can afford to pay for these learning skills from education sources outside the normal school environment.

To permit students access to their highest level of possible success and potential, all students must learn these learning skills. Is that not the basic and fundamental purpose for the concept of school? Why should schools give students basic clay or artist canvas, without also giving them the brushes, paint, molds and guides to form that clay and to paint those pictures?

Is the reluctance by schools to teach these most valuable skills caused by lack of knowledge, lack of concern, lack of motivation or lack of ability? Or, is this reluctance caused by the apprehension that the school system might really become too successful—and would require less attention for political causes and budget emphasis?

Learning to learn, the topic discussed above, is the first task in the personal success process for students—guided and encouraged by their parents. The second task for students and parents to improve the education process is to become proactive in the policy and administrative process. That important task will be reviewed next.

Direct Parent and Student Involvement

Parents and students have the ability and the power to force the education system to be improved. If they ask enough questions based on the information in this book, or based on their personal knowledge and preferences, administrators and political leaders must eventually be forced to acknowledge and to respond to those questions.

Parents and students—particularly students—should write letters to their education administrators, their legislators and their governors. They should write many letters. They should write tons of letters. Their voices and their letters might be the only real fire and heat to get any positive action, other than the usual common rhetoric, from responsible leaders. Political leaders are sensitive to public opinion, especially a tidal wave of public opinion. There are enough students in this country, in any state or even in any school district to create a tidal wave of letters that would stop useless political rhetoric "dead in its tracks." Once that useless and confusing rhetoric is halted, positive and measurable education purposes and goals might be determined.

For ease and convenience in writing letters, the following sample letter is presented as a guide. It may be used as a guide, or if the letter writer chooses to use this sample letter directly, the author gives permission for this letter to be copied. This letter may also be altered for use by a parent.

Sample letter:

Dear (Honorable) _____

My name is _____. I am a student at_____.
I am a mature and responsible student who feels that the education environment and our current education system are not helping to create good education results for many students. I would like to express my personal concern to you, and make some suggestions that I believe will make the education process more effective.

Our social and political environment discourages positive and progressive education, and the education system itself seems to be designed to accommodate weak and uninspired students. The education system is not designed to offer higher challenges and opportunities for inspired students.

I also believe that the current education system does not help those weaker students who need different types of programs other than basic academic programs. They need different programs that will allow them to function productively within their capabilities without destroying their self-esteem.

In my local area, I have observed the following problems with my school system:

1. (Do not use money as a problem)
2. (List problems clearly and individually)
3.

I recommend the following actions to solve those problems to help make our education process more effective—to the needs of society, and to my needs as a student who wants an opportunity for a more rewarding education:

1. (Do not use money as a solution)
2. (List suggestions clearly and individually)
3.

Please give these ideas and suggestions your serious and urgent consideration. Please remember that I and all my classmates are the hope for the future of our country, and I hope to have at least the same opportunity that you have for a successful and fulfilling life.

Thank you for taking time to read this letter. I also thank you in advance for any positive interest and action that you will take.

Respectfully,

(Your name)

Students are free people in this free society. It's their right even as students to have their opinions heard, especially when the question or the problem directly concerns their future and their success. If students don't personally take positive actions to make their future better for themselves that positive action will most likely never be taken. Our society has become accustomed to answering education problems with more and louder rhetoric. Leaders simply "talk the problem to death."

No definite action that's produced significantly measurable results in the education process has been taken in recent history.

Summary

Students, as well as anyone who wants to become successful, must learn the process of achieving success. There's a definite pattern, or plan, to success. It's not something that "just happens." Students are taught reading, writing and arithmetic. They are told that if they learn the three "Rs" well and work hard that they will become successful.

Certainly the three "Rs" and hard work are essential parts of becoming successful, but they aren't necessarily the most important parts. There are many brilliant people who aren't successful. Everybody knows one or more of those persons. There are also many hard-working people who aren't successful. Everybody knows one or more of those persons also. Why are these brilliant minds wasted, and why are those hard-working people only tired and frustrated? The answer is because they never learned the success process.

The tragedy of this waste and lost aspirations of those who can become successful but don't is that the success process is simple and easy to learn. It's also tragic that this process is not a taught process. It's not on the school curriculum. It's merely assumed that if anyone knows enough of the basics, of the three "R's", that he or she will eventually figure out, by sheer luck or accident, the success process.

Students cannot afford to ignore learning the success process so they can use that information and their other skills to become successful. They should encourage their teachers and principals to begin a success planning curriculum in their schools, so that no students are ignored.

If students believe this can happen and take only one positive step—many times—to make it happen, then it will eventually happen. Norman Vincent Peale advises, "When tackling a problem the number one thing is, never quit attacking it."[10] Success training should not be ignored in society, especially in schools, any longer.

CHAPTER NINE

SUCCESS AND MOTIVATION OBSTACLES

Although a student, or anyone else, must have a definite success plan to become successful, the mere possession of that plan doesn't automatically assure one of becoming successful. The success plan is the positive force. There are also negative forces that tend to work against one's success plan. These negative forces are obstacles to success. If there were no obstacles to success, everyone would be successful. Since these obstacles keep many people from becoming successful these obstacles must be identified so they may be avoided. A student, or anyone else, who's not aware of the negative forces of these obstacles might be defeated by these obstacles without realizing the cause of that defeat.

Motivation efforts and techniques have been devised in a manner to suggest that the recipient of those efforts is in a vacuum, isolated from efforts that would influence that person in a negative direction. Motivationists have offered positive guidance, but they haven't offered complementary guidance to defend against those negative influences which, in many situations, are stronger than those positive motivation efforts.

To defend against obstacles to success and motivation, one must understand the existence and nature of these obstacles. Obstacles and barriers to success must be identified and analyzed to understand how to build a protective defense against those negative influences. Those major obstacles will be analyzed here. They include:

- Cultural deprivation
- Peer pressure

- Group loyalty
- Lack of self-confidence
- Fear of making mistakes
- Ambivalence—Lack of focus
- Unclear guidelines
- Social influences
- Drug abuse
- Health abuse
- Dropping out of school

Each of these obstacles is powerful enough, individually, to deter or prevent a person from performing according to his or her success plan. Combined, their negative influence becomes insurmountable for many less inspired persons. These obstacles usually aren't isolated, for they ordinarily function together.

Each of these obstacles will be briefly analyzed to understand their influence. Students and their parents must learn to identify these obstacles and they must also learn to be mutually supportive to maintain a positive success plan.

Cultural Deprivation

Students ordinarily identified as culturally deprived are those students from the lower social and economic classes who have no closely associated successful role models. They are from families accustomed to hardship and despair. Those families have no aspirations that would be a basis to make the work ethic or the study ethic seem logical. They are waiting for someone to give them an opportunity; however, they realize that any opportunity is only a matter of false hopes for themselves, so those other privileged people can grab more.

Although their intelligence levels might be very high, their personalities are very narrow, which keeps them from objectively trying to understand situations, conditions and alternatives. They tend to interpret all situations around them as attempts to discredit, exploit or to take advantage of them—because of their status. Many carry a "chip on their shoulder."

The real potential of many culturally deprived people is often hidden behind a hard mask that they wear to defend themselves. To develop that hidden potential, leaders and parents must become aware of those sensitivities and guide those students toward removal of those defensive masks—by themselves.

Those defensive masks are the visible products of the cultural obstacle. Listed below are actions that will assist a concerned teacher or parent to develop the potential that many of those students possess. A parent from a low cultural environment might need to learn these ideas while teaching them:

1. Status is dominant in that student's thoughts. That student anticipates comments that would indicate an insult, a "put down," or an insinuation that he or she is not as "good" as other people.
2. A teacher should make frequent small talk with that student. The parent should always offer encouragement.
3. The teacher should encourage student participation during group discussions.
4. The teacher and parent should assign more progressively difficult tasks to that child.
5. Teachers and parents should habitually give that person a pat on the back, if it can reasonably be justified.

The purpose for this directed training is to help the student learn that he or she is a normal person with normal intelligence, normal abilities and normal opportunities. This is a form of operant conditioning identified by B. F. Skinner with teachers and parents reinforcing positive behavior and ideas.

Peer Pressure

Peer pressure is the meanest and most destructive obstacle to overcome, for it's a force that inhibits a student, or any other person, from doing what that person really needs to do and wants to do.

This negative force, this obstacle of peer pressure, has no special targets. It attacks negative students, casual students, students who want to be successful and students who are positive and successful. Peer pressure actually forces weaker-willed students to be unsuccessful, and attempts to make stronger students feel guilty for their extra achievement.

Actions to eliminate the peer pressure obstacle cannot be casual and subtle. Direct and open actions are required by the person who chooses to remove this obstacle, to allow students to develop their own self-motivation. Students who recognize the force of peer pressure may reject it themselves. Otherwise this corrective action must be encouraged by parents with added reinforcement and training by teachers. These actions include the following: (Leader refers to parents or teachers.)

1. A leader should expose the peer pressure monster by training of its use and effect.
2. A leader should encourage striving students who might be under strong negative pressures.

3. A leader should enforce strong disciplinary action against anyone who openly and conspicuously tries to decrease the performance and success of another person in that environment.

There are two fundamental purposes for these actions. First is to encourage an inherently self-motivated person to allow his or her motivation to develop, so that person may become as successful as aspirations will permit. Secondly, is to instill in the study environment that negative peer pressure is a clear and planned violation of acceptable discipline that will not be tolerated.

Group Loyalty

Group loyalty is another serious obstacle that restricts or prevents positive results from motivation efforts. Group loyalty may appear the same as peer pressure; however, there are subtle differences that separate these two forces.

Peer pressure is a psychological force placed upon someone by others. The force is usually negative in nature, but there are some positive aspects, occasionally; especially when peer pressure applies to athletics and other normal group activities with a shared and clear goal.

Group loyalty, on the other hand, is represented by a willing acceptance by an individual of the desired group. In this case the individual is the initiator, striving for group membership. To be accepted by the group, the individual is responsible to conform to group norms and group expectations. There's a pressure influence, but it's self-imposed by an individual to maintain the feeling of belonging to a secure group.

Low Confidence Level

Many people, including students, cannot motivate themselves for they don't have enough self-confidence in their abilities or their potential. Although a low self-confidence level would seem to be a result of cultural deprivation, this is not the only source of low self-confidence. Cultural deprivation is only one source.

Low self-confidence may result from other life experiences and emotional events. It could be based upon real or imagined situations. It could even exist for no apparent reason. Some examples of possible sources of low self-confidence are:

- The birth order of siblings
- The level of comfort in the home environment

- The attention given to a young child
- The encouragement offered by authority figures
- The determination level of a person

All these factors, and many others, are the basis for perceptions. A person's confidence level is determined by the perception an individual has of himself or herself.

That person might have strong aspirations, and understand the needs and desires to do something. That person might also have clearly defined goals that are definite. That person might have the perfect success plan. All these prerequisites, however, are irrelevant if that person isn't motivated to act—to achieve those things. The corrective approach for the low self-confidence student is basically the same as that required for the culturally deprived student. It must be nurtured by the parent and reinforced by the teacher.

Many people are afraid of failure, therefore, they refuse to do anything that would create that risk. This lack of ability to take some degree of risk often results in naturally safe failure. One cannot be criticized for failing when one does nothing.

To overcome this fear obstacle, students should learn to build confidence by practicing little wins. Parents should praise their children for those natural little wins to reinforce the concept that little wins are success and that failure is only a temporary hesitation that may be readjusted. A failure is not permanent—it's only an opportunity to do something else.

Fear of Mistakes

Some students, even those who are highly confident, are fearful of making mistakes. They might fear that a mistake will indicate they are stupid, a mistake will compromise their credibility, a mistake will jeopardize their career or a mistake will make them appear only human. Whatever the reason for the fear of making mistakes, that reluctance to do something will cause a person to appear unmotivated. This reluctance may be seen as a natural tendency to reject motivation.

Assisting and coaching students not to fear mistakes requires special skills. The teacher or parent must understand the subtle differences in acceptable and unacceptable mistakes—and be able to communicate those differences to students in a way to create mutual understanding, as well as mutual confidence. Simply explaining the results of different types and degrees of mistakes will have no positive effect if the student doesn't trust or respect the judgement of the parent or teacher. This correction process should proceed as follows:

1. The leader should explain that there are basically two types of mistakes—one is the learning mistake and the other is the attention mistake. Learning mistakes are acceptable for a short period of time during indoctrination, but should decrease when the person is more experienced.
2. The attention mistake is one that's repeated from one's inability to concentrate, or from one's disinterest in a subject or an action.
3. The leader should then teach the student from that concept.

Ambivalence—Lack of Focus

Another significant obstacle to a student's motivation is the absence of a success plan. Motivation may occur only when one has a need to be fulfilled. If a person cannot recognize a need, or doesn't have a clear plan or idea of how to satisfy that need, then the person is faced with a vague and self-imposed obstacle. The lack of an identifiable goal, a success plan, makes it impossible to reach that goal.

This is an obstacle that's the basic source of disappointment and conflict in most environments. Leaders become frustrated because they cannot find a way to help motivate their workers who suffer from this influence; and those workers become frustrated and disenchanted in the workplace because they feel that they aren't successful.

Parents and teachers become frustrated when students cannot be motivated to develop themselves. Students become frustrated for they don't know what they want to do.

To be eliminated, this obstacle requires a person with special skills since this is the obstacle that might be the most dominant in most environments—and it remains unrecognized. The parent, or teacher, must be a good coach and must understand the success-planning process. Only a brief outline of the success-planning process will be given here, since that process is explained in another chapter. The success-planning process includes:

1. A complete understanding of goal differentiation
2. Learning to develop successful attitudes
3. Remaining determined and focused
4. A commitment to self-development
5. Avoiding frustrations
6. Improving communications skills
7. Enhancing interpersonal relationships

Each of these subjects is important in the success process for an individual. Not only are they the "secrets to success," they are also necessary to help one remain focused on a purpose.

Unclear Guidelines or Models

Some people, including students, often have the success obstacle of an unclear guideline or an unclear objective placed in their path to success. This is usually caused by unclear communications based on the assumption that the student, or the person, knows concepts and ideas that the authority person understands—which might not be a valid assumption.

Parents should give clear information to their children when offering serious guidance. That information, or that instruction, should not be coded with alternative conclusions or innuendo that might create ambivalence or misinterpretation. If the parent isn't sure of correct information or guidance, that parent should get correct information from a reliable source—and it should be clear.

The student also has a responsibility for correct information and guidance. If the student is unclear or uncertain about the meaning of information or guidance, that student must make his or her uncertainty known. That student must ask for more information to remove that ambivalence. How can one do something effectively if he or she doesn't know what to do?

Social Influences

Society creates major obstacles to student learning and, eventually, to worker productivity. Educators traditionally emphasize that students cannot be adequately taught without more money for education. If adequate money is not available, are we and students to assume that students are not adequately taught? Is this assumption not a direct obstacle that a student must consciously overcome to concentrate effectively on learning to study?

Business and industrial leaders habitually bemoan the inadequacy and lack of skills of modern students. Education administrators react to this criticism with more criticism of their own education systems. Should they not first question the motives and the competence of those leaders who make those allegations? It's possible that much of the business and industrial criticism of new workers—products of the education system—is simply to cover their own weaknesses and inadequacies to offer real motivational and training opportunities for those new workers?

To overcome this obstacle, parents and students must concentrate on the individual task at hand. They must not be influenced by rhetoric and excuses of other interests. They must remain focused on their one individual success plan and have confidence that that success plan will work for them—personally.

A Special Success Problem—Drugs

To become successful, there's another serious obstacle that many students must consider. That's the avoidance of harmful drugs. (And, perhaps even helping with the eradication of harmful drugs from our society.) Students are probably aware of the usual reasons for avoiding drugs. These are often cited as: psychological disorders, legal problems, harm to one's body and even death.

There's another problem that affects students, whether they use drugs or not. This is the economic problem. When illegal drugs are sold, much of the money to buy those drugs leaves the money supply of our economy. The money supply, our economic base, declines. This means that opportunities for economic and financial success are reduced for everyone. The drug sellers have stolen that money and part of the economic base from students.

Even students who have enough success focus to avoid drug use, personally, must still get involved in the eradication of that problem. How can students do this? They must report drug pushers who operate on their school grounds, or who associate with student groups. Of course it's difficult to get involved with these events for that action takes much self-confidence and courage. Students must act from a concerned strength of character to do what must be done. At this point some questions must be asked of individual students to emphasize the importance of this task:

- If you saw someone point a gun at a student, and shoot that student—would you report that incident? Or, would you be afraid to get involved?
- If you saw someone steal a purse from a student that you know—would you report that incident? Or, would you be afraid to get involved?
- Would you have the personal strength of character to do what you know is right and just. Or, would you be afraid to get involved?
- Does right and justice have any meaning for students—or is that just an adult requirement?

A drug dealer, or pusher, is no more harmless than the person who would shoot a student or steal from a student. Furthermore, a drug dealer is stealing from the future of all people, especially students. Students who would protect a friend who's a drug dealer are their own worst enemies. They are also serious menaces to their other friends for they refuse to protect them.

Student Health

Health of students plays a major role in the success of students. Bad health is an obstacle to the success of an otherwise capable student. This factor is often ignored, which results in a condition that might be assumed to be lack of motivation or lack of concern. Student health should be considered from two dimensions. These include physical health and emotional health.

Physical health is often discussed and analyzed. Emotional health is not, for it's usually assumed that an emotional crisis of a student results from "growing up." These two health problems will be discussed briefly only as a reminder of their importance in the learning and success process.

The best intentions of planning for success are often defeated by neglect of student health. An unhealthy student, even with a high level of desire and motivation, might not achieve his or her maximum goals. Although good health is vital to a good study program, it's often ignored and not considered as an important factor. Most often, study weakness is attributed to the lack of ability or lack of interest. Health factors, although usually ignored, play a major role in the learning process.

Physical exercise is considered the most important health deficiency of students. Studies indicate that the brain works at higher efficiency if it has a good blood supply with plenty of oxygen. A person who doesn't exercise sufficiently deprives his or her brain, and body, of at least some needed oxygen. Authorities suggest that as many as forty percent of men students and seventy percent of women students fail to get enough exercise to provide a sufficient oxygen flow.[5] This includes even the failure of many students to walk enough—perhaps we have too many automobiles?

Sleep is also important to maintain a healthy body and mind that can perform tasks required for study. Between six and nine hours of restful sleep are required for most people to perform at their best. Sleep allows the body to release toxins, to repair tissue damage and to store energy for the next day's activities. To gain the most benefit from sleep, good sleep habits should be developed: prepare to go to bed the same way, and at the same time.

Diet is another important health factor. The effects of food and nutrition are too expansive to be discussed adequately in this brief article; furthermore, there are many sources available that cover diet and nutrition. However, some important general guidelines include the following:

1. A diet must contain proper proportions of vitamins, minerals, carbohydrates, proteins and WATER.
2. Increased exercise may compensate for a diet that's too high in calories. This problem may remain hidden until the exercise diminishes.
3. Avoid white sugar, it's considered a dead food.
4. Some people may be allergic to Aspartame (Nutrasweet) and aren't aware of it. It may cause vision problems, and may even cause negative personality changes such as irritability and aggression. (See a medical doctor for specific information and guidance.)
5. DRINK AT LEAST 40 OUNCES OF WATER EACH DAY. This does not mean tea, soda or beer. Water is the only drink that flushes toxins from one's body.

Alcohol and drugs damage a person's (student's) ability to rationalize and think logically. Prolonged use may even do permanent damage to brain cells. Killed brain cells don't regenerate. A student who abuses these substances will most likely not be able to reach his or her maximum level of potential, for that potential will eventually be destroyed by lack of success-focus, lack of concentration and lack of self-esteem.

Emotional health of a student is often ignored. A student who has emotional or personality problems is normally considered to have a disciplinary problem, or as merely a child with an immaturity problem. Parents shouldn't automatically make this assumption, for a child who routinely exhibits unusual or antisocial characteristics could be suffering from serious emotional or psychological problems.

Later in this section, some normal defensive mechanisms to frustration will be identified. These traits routinely occur for short periods as reactions to normal frustrations. If these traits occur only occasionally, the child is most likely reacting to normal frustration. On the other hand, if these traits or more serious traits exhibit themselves consistently within a child, that child's emotional condition should be evaluated by a professional. An emotional problem can be a serious obstacle to a student's success, and shouldn't be ignored.

Dropping Out of School

A student who drops out of school personally and intentionally creates his or her greatest obstacle to becoming successful. One who drops out of school certainly discredits himself or herself and that person's family. That discreditation is a voluntary act that condemns a person to future embarrassment, reluctance to participate in many meaningful social and civic activities, and inability to take advantage of opportunities that more educated persons would accept as normal. The school dropout condemns himself or herself to "second classhood." Perhaps that person might become financially comfortable, but that lowered self-image will remain a barrier to a feeling of personal fulfillment.

The dropout also discredits his or her family. Although that person is an individual with personal hopes, dreams and aspirations, he or she is also part of a family grouping that within itself has hopes, dreams and aspirations. Anything a student does directly affects that student's family regardless of the level of love, affection or compatibility within that family. A student cannot totally isolate or disassociate himself or herself from his or her family. That related family exists as an important part of a person because those physical and emotional genes are connected.

The status of friendships and peer relationships should also be considered by a student before he or she decides to quit school. Of course the absence of close friends in school might be one of the reasons that would encourage a susceptible student to quit school; however, the lack of friendships is usually for only a short duration. The effect on one's friends must be considered.

If one's friends continue their education and graduate from high school, that puts them into a different category from that of the dropout. Their graduation, or the act of continuing their education, places them into a category of "winners." One who quits, or drops out, places himself or herself into the category of "quitters" or "losers." This separation of social status and categories of winners and losers will sever those friendships.

Real winners have no reason, inclination or time to waste associating with losers. This is a rather harsh statement, and in rare cases, might not be totally accurate. However, it's a valid and important observation that should be dealt with logically. A winner likes to associate with winners. They share the same ideals, goals and aspirations. Consequently, they have the same reference points upon which to build and sustain close relationships. They encourage each other and support each other toward those reference points.

A loser cannot remain within this close grouping for his or her self-image, and the image of him or her by friends, will not permit these reference points to be basic foundations for relationships. Those positive reference points become clouded when a loser or quitter is within that winner's circle. The result is that the dropout, or quitter, will lose friends, not because they feel that they are "better," but because those basic reference points are changed.

If a student chooses to drop out of school that student voluntarily chooses to be less than he or she can be. That student voluntarily chooses to lower his or her self-image, his or her confidence and his or her potential for a more comfortable and rewarding life. That student voluntarily chooses to accept fifty years of hardship and frustration, to escape only two or three years of minor discomfort in school. This doesn't seem to be the tradeoff that a rational person would make.

The dropout student will most likely add to the economic burden of government and taxpayers by that selfish act of dropping out of school. That actual level of economic damage probably cannot be calculated for each individual; however, multiplied by the total numbers of high school dropouts, the damage is significant. Even when the low wage earner, or the zero wage earner, doesn't burden society with demands and expectations of welfare support—the alternative lifestyle—that person remains a burden for he or she doesn't contribute anything to help the economic foundation of society.

The realistic and essential challenge for any at risk or discouraged student is to continue and to complete his or her education. It's particularly important to get at least a high school diploma. Trying to get a good job, or any reasonable job for that matter, without a high school diploma is almost impossible. Many industries will not even consider an application for employment if the applicant doesn't have a high school diploma.

Without a high school diploma one is severely handicapped in the job market. That person's hands are tied behind his or her back while trying to row upstream, blindfolded, in the job market. One's progress and success opportunities will be extremely limited and restricted by facing these handicaps.

Summary—Obstacles

These obstacles to education, motivation and success are powerful forces that limit the level of success that a person might reasonably expect to attain. Students and their parents must learn to recognize these obstacles, their causes and effects to allow themselves the opportunity to begin positive and corrective actions before these potential obstacles become real obstacles. Once either of these obstacles becomes part of a student's normal culture and aspirations that obstacle becomes more difficult to overcome, for it's accepted more as a fact of normal life rather than an obstacle that's creeped into one's life.

Students and their parents must be constantly vigilant to guard against these obstacles. No one else can do that for them. To help in this vigilance, there are some indicators to show when an obstacle is causing a negative influence. Those obstacles will normally create student frustrations. Those frustrations are the first signs of obstacles. Defensive reactions to those frustrations—the first visible signals—will be identified and explained next.

Defensive Reactions to Frustrations

Obstacles to success cause many observable reactions by people, including students. Many of these reactions are identified as defensive mechanisms to frustrations caused by those obstacles. These defensive mechanisms include:[19]

Withdrawal

The person who suffers from withdrawal doesn't participate in the normal activities of his or her organization. This condition is applicable in all environments, but it's especially applicable in a work environment and a school environment. In a work environment the person's withdrawal would ordinarily concern only the workplace if the person's frustrations were created from conditions in the workplace. Unless that person had other problems this condition wouldn't be dominant in other environments such as the home environment. Ordinarily, a worker suffering from withdrawal in the workplace would have more rewarding and compensating interests in other environments.

A student, on the other hand, might be affected somewhat differently. A student trying to avoid frustration might exhibit withdrawal in many environments since students often have fewer major interests, such as family responsibilities. The absence of multiple major interests and responsibilities doesn't allow them other areas in which to compensate for their frustrations when an obstacle is encountered in another area.

When a student becomes frustrated, embarrassed or disappointed that student should discuss those frustrations with someone who can provide comfort and encouragement. That student's parent must be prepared and ready to occupy that role. If not, that parent should find someone who can.

Most parents are aware of mood changes, especially withdrawal, in their children. They should become involved as soon as this unusual behavior is noticed.

Aggression

An aggressive person normally would be quite conspicuous. This person would be sensitive, touchy, and easily angered. The aggression could be displayed against acquaintances, authority figures or even society in general. The source of aggressive behavior in a child, student, must be known before any effective actions could be taken by a parent. Some aggression is normal behavior by a child, under certain situations. For example, when a child becomes annoyed or angry with a sibling or an antagonizing friend.

The key to determining unusual aggression must come from understanding the normal behavior of the child under certain conditions. Aggression by a child in a situation that doesn't ordinarily cause aggressive behavior by that child would indicate the possibility of unusual obstacles, problems and frustration. The parent, or the teacher, must know the student well enough to identify any unusual aggressive behavior. Once the source of aggressiveness is determined the parent, and the teacher under some conditions, must help the child solve the problem.

Substitution

If a student (or a worker if in a job environment) cannot satisfy his or her needs within the normal environment, that person may substitute, or seek to fulfill those needs, in another area outside the normal environment. Students who cannot find a feeling of belonging or a sense of esteem in their school environment often seek another environment that will provide those basic needs. These basic needs are described by Maslow in Chapter Four.

For example, a student with high intelligence and abilities might dislike or ignore the school environment if that student is ignored in that environment, is not recognized for achievements in that environment or has no friends in that environment. In this case, that student might be encouraged to focus more on a job environment or a social environment that would provide those basic needs. This is probably one of the major conditions that causes students to quit school or to ignore their studies. Many high school dropouts are intelligent children—who aren't aware of their abilities.

Compensation

The person reacting to frustration by compensation would concentrate more strongly in one activity or specialize in one area or function to make up, or compensate, for an unfulfilled need in a desired area. For example, a student who becomes frustrated with a difficult academic course might put his or her total effort toward becoming an excellent artist or a good musician. This is not to suggest that all artists and musicians result from frustration with academics, for there are many artists and musicians who choose to be what they are as their first, or natural, choice.

The defensive mechanism of compensation suggests that when an obstacle interferes with a person's focused goal, extraordinary efforts may be placed on a secondary goal. The secondary goal may be as important and as rewarding as the original goal. Frustration might remain, however, since the person failed to reach the original goal.

Repression

Some people intentionally forget, or lose awareness of a problem that's caused by frustration to reach a goal or to fulfill a need. They cannot solve the obstacle, so they simply convince themselves that it doesn't exist or that it isn't important enough to consider.

In the case of a student, one might consider the concept of failing grades. If a student believes that he or she cannot improve scores in a certain subject, that student under the influence of repression might intentionally ignore that subject and consider those grades as not existing.

Projection

The defensive mechanism of projection causes one to assume another's feelings or thoughts as a justification for failure to overcome an obstacle. In this case the person doesn't accept the responsibility for the results of his or her actions or efforts. Examples, used frequently, include:

"The teacher hates me! That's why I failed."
"My parents hate me! How can I feel normal?"
"Nobody likes me, so I can't possibly succeed."
"I would have made it—but it wasn't in the cards."

One who uses projection blames failure on something else or someone else. That person assumes that it's not his or her fault. Projection voids that personal responsibility.

Rationalization

If the problem or obstacle cannot be solved, there must be a logical and socially acceptable reason for the person's failure or lack of good performance. A logical reason sounds better than an admission of low performance, and it helps to protect one's self-image. Typical examples within education are:

"I just didn't have time to study for the test."

"The test didn't cover the taught material."

"I had a headache during the test."

"The teacher doesn't know how to teach this course."

These are typical comments from students who have difficulty with certain subjects or tests. This rationalization even has more validity when comments are based on common belief or partial truth.

Summary

These defensive mechanisms are recognizable in most organizations, in most families and in most social entities. These defensive characteristics aren't necessarily the result of weak motivation programs or techniques. Neither are they necessarily the result of bad employees, children, students or other people. These negative and defensive responses result from frustration to those motivation obstacles. Those obstacles are more powerful than most leaders' and parents' ability to apply positive motivation techniques.

These obstacles must be resolved before positive motivation may be influenced. To attempt traditional motivation techniques without reducing these obstacles will continue to create frustration for everyone in the work environment, in the school environment, in the home environment and in society.

The next chapter discusses the concept of demotivation, which may be an important concept in helping a student learn how to succeed. Although the concept of demotivation might sound similar to the concept of obstacles discussed in this chapter, it's not. Obstacles are those real things that often must be overcome or defeated. Demotivation is a condition that must be removed internally by a person, by understanding perceptions and emotional reactions.

CHAPTER TEN

AVOIDING DEMOTIVATION

Chapter Four, which analyzed motivation, discussed history, theory, efforts and techniques for one person to affect the motivation of another person. That information gave a basis for direct motivation efforts, but those suggestions also contain the implication that one person might not be able to influence, directly, the motivation of another person.

Possibly, motivation is a trait or an influence that's internally generated by each individual for his or her own use as his or her perceptions guide that person. If this consideration is valid, then a different approach must be considered for the motivation process. Although a new approach must be considered, it must continue to be reinforced by those traditional motivation concepts. Neither can be ignored, since motivation is a dynamic yet vague concept. Perhaps a new motivation theory should be considered that's in reverse of itself. This theory would be considered the "Demotivation Theory." This theory would be based upon the following concept:

MOTIVATION CANNOT BE DIRECTLY PLANNED OR FORCED UPON SOMEONE. THE CONCEPT IS TO REMOVE DEMOTIVATORS AND BARRIERS FROM THE ENVIRONMENT TO PERMIT MOTIVATION.

The basis for this concept might be formed from a combination of ideas, two of which have already been presented. These include Herzberg's Two-Factor theory, discussed in Chapter Four; Piaget's studies that were mentioned in Chapter One and Douglas McGregor's identification of leadership approaches.[20]

McGregor suggested that leaders function on the basis of two approaches. One, Theory X, is that workers are basically lazy, uninspired and must be forced to be productive. The other approach, Theory Y, is that workers are self-motivated, desire to be useful and productive and need only an opportunity to prove themselves. McGregor's Theory Y adds further support to the idea that motivation is a natural occurrence—if allowed to exist. Although McGregor, as well as Herzberg, considered only the work environment in promoting their concepts and theories, these concepts may apply equally well to students in the education environment. Students are also real people. They respond to motivations in similar ways to fulfill needs as do workers, since most needs are universal in nature.

From this assimilation of theories, the following theory evolves as a basis to improve a student's volition, or natural choice, to participate more actively in the education process:

PEOPLE HAVE A NATURAL INCLINATION TO BE MOTI-VATED. THEY WILL FOLLOW THAT NATURAL INCLINATION IF DEMOTIVATORS AND BARRIERS ARE REMOVED FROM THEIR FUNCTIONING ENVIRONMENT.

This concept offers a more direct and practical approach for a student to motivate himself or herself—and for a parent to assist in that motivation process. A parent, teacher or anyone else involved with the education process should simply remove demotivators and obstacles then allow a student to find his or her natural motivation. Naturally, for this approach to produce results the student must be one who understands personal responsibility. Under the demotivation approach the student is responsible for his or her motivation. However, parents must still guide and encourage those students. Laziness and procrastination are always huge temptations even to the most disciplined and motivated people, including adults.

A Demotivation Theory—The Natural Approach

To consider a practical motivation process, whereby everyone may achieve a higher probability of fulfilling their obligations and responsibilities to themselves, to their groups and to their society, there are two important universal questions. They are:

1. CAN ANYONE REALLY BE MOTIVATED?
2. HOW CAN IT BE DONE?

The remainder of this chapter helps to answer these two questions. To begin this understanding let's use a typical example that occurs everyday in the average workplace. A workplace example is used for its obvious clarity. Similar conditions in the education environment are more subtle.

When people begin a job, they start the job already motivated. They wanted the job, they applied for the job, and they were prepared to accept the job. At that time, they were looking forward to earning money, buying things they needed and wanted, being part of a new environment and doing the best job they could, so their families and supervisors would be proud of them. Nobody had to encourage them or give them a two week detailed course on the subject of motivation. All they needed was an opportunity to show what they could do.

Some of those workers, three to six months later, show no concern or respect for their jobs. What happened? They became demotivated.

If they were demotivated, how did it happen? Whose fault was it? The answer—they could have become demotivated by themselves, or they could have been demotivated by actions or inactions of leaders.

Who's the biggest loser if a worker becomes demotivated? Both are the biggest losers. Leaders lose productivity and profit and workers lose esteem, pride and progressive careers.

The same concept of demotivation influences students in the education environment. Students who need and desire esteem are naturally motivated to seek that esteem. Since the desire for esteem is a universal need, it must be considered that most normal students seek esteem. Therefore, most normal students should be motivated to seek that esteem. One of the methods to achieve esteem in the school environment is to make good grades. Another way is to be popular; however, even popular students who don't make good grades tend to become less popular.

To understand the demotivation concept, it's necessary to identify and understand those demotivators. They will be analyzed next.

The Demotivators

There are two types or sources of demotivation. These are internal sources and external sources—from the viewpoint of the individual—worker or student. Internal demotivators include the following:

- Comparing oneself to others
- Failing to establish personal goals
- Yielding to frustration and lack of confidence
- Ignoring health and energy needs
- Making work last longer
- Distrusting authority figures
- Losing the desire to be number one

- Focusing on jealousy or revenge
- Focusing on unrelated problems

External sources of demotivation include:

- Not having clear organizational goals or expectations
- Not given adequate responsibility
- Weak or no training in the organization
- Being isolated from the informal organization
- Poor leadership in the organization
- A bad work or school environment
- No appreciation or respect from authority figures
- Constantly changing practices or policies

These same demotivators that apply in the workplace for workers also apply in the education environment and home environment for children. Children, like workers, come into their environments full of excitement, anticipation and motivation. A child is naturally motivated to learn to talk, crawl, walk and learn. Many parents of children between the ages of three and five suffer two or three years of continuous frustration, trying to answer only one question from naturally motivated children. That constant question is, "Why?"

Some children maintain that motivation throughout their lifetimes—others become demotivated, and suddenly become subjects of motivation concerns for families, local economic areas and society in general. These who suffer the effects of demotivation not only fail to become personally successful, they ordinarily become burdens to society.

A selected few of the more common sources of demotivation will be analyzed individually to demonstrate their effects.

These will be analyzed by associating their effects on workers in the work environment with their effects on students in education and home environments. Most parents now work in the work environment, so they should quickly observe this relative association.

Let's first consider the internal sources of demotivation. Internal demotivators are those that a person generates within his or her own thought processes.

Comparing Oneself to Others

Do the following comments sound familiar? "I have to do everything because Joe never does anything around here." "I never get caught up, and he's always fooling around." "I wish he would at least do his fair share." "Since he gets paid more than I do, I'm not going to do any more than he does."

Most people have heard these comments, or comments simiar to these, in most environments—especially in every work environment. The purpose for this analysis is not to make a judgement on whether this is a true or fair situation. Maybe the person making those comments is absolutely correct in his or her observation. Maybe he or she is associated with a co-worker who's lazy, or who doesn't have the physical or mental ability to do well at that job. That doesn't matter, for this discussion pertains to the response and action of the person who makes comparisons of performance and fairness.

When the other person was hired into the job, was there an actual or implied understanding, between the employee and employer, that the employee would work in the same way, and at the same pace, as everybody else? Did the employee indicate that he or she would compare performance, and work only to the level that would equal the pay he or she would get?

Of course not. When an applicant accepts a job it must be with the explicit or implied agreement that he or she will give the best performance, based upon his or her abilities and expectations, and that the employee accepts the pay rate for doing that job. The employee has the duty and commitment to do the best that he or she can, and the employer has a duty and legal obligation to pay the employee what was agreed.

The employee doesn't have the arbitrary right to give less performance, and the employer doesn't have the arbitrary right to give less pay, because he or she knows another employer who pays less for the same job. Each have equal obligations and equal commitments. A good employee, planning a successful career, certainly wouldn't fail to meet his or her obligations for an irrelevant reason such as comparing performances.

A leader may also be the source of external demotivation by comparing a worker's performance with another worker. Any comparison of and between workers is hazardous to esteem and motivation.

Now, let's compare this normal workplace situation with a student's situation. Remember—students are real people with real feelings and emotions too.

Children, as well as workers, demotivate themselves by comparing their abilities, their intelligence and how they look, with other children. A child who feels that he or she is not as capable in an activity as another child will tend to avoid that activity to prevent the embarrassment and ridicule from other children. Once the avoidance practice begins that becomes a normal activity for that child.

If a child feels that he or she is not as "smart" as other children, that child might avoid situations where those comparisons might be made. In the extreme cases, the child even skips classes or drops out of school to avoid this embarrassment. It's even possible that the child who fails might be more intelligent than others who are the basis for the comparison, since grades depend upon study habits as well as basic intelligence.

During adolescent years, the comparison of physical appearance becomes a more dynamic influence that forces children to do things that appear abnormal, but which actually are natural reactions. One example is when a child is shunned by his or her peers for what he or she considers ugliness. That child might have difficulty to maintain his or her natural motivation, even if he or she develops into the most handsome adult.

Another example is that of girls who fail gym and athletic classes. Many girls fear having to shower and dress with a group of other girls who they think have more beautiful "physical attributes."

Having no Goals Established

An employee who has no firm definite goals established will certainly find it easy to develop self-demotivation. Why should that employee be working with diligence if that person doesn't understand what he or she is working for? A person must be working to achieve something either tangible or something psychological. If an employee cannot relate the job to things such as more comfort, more prestige, a better car, a savings account, nice clothes, being "number one" on the job, or planning for retirement, then that employee will eventually create self-demotivation.

This is probably the most fundamental form of internal demotivation, for there's no common perception to use as a reference point to regain lost motivation. If the employee has been "getting by" without having to work effectively for a purpose, then that employee will probably be content to keep on "just getting by." To this person, the loss of the job would probably not be very traumatic, for the employee could keep "just getting by" without having to work. In fact, only the loss of the job may help that employee identify some goals and a purpose.

Students are similarly affected by their lack of clear goals. A student who doesn't understand why he or she should be a successful student has no logical reason to remain motivated to be a successful student—perhaps other than to avoid punishment. Once the child is mature or develops a rebellious attitude, however, punishment and threats lose their effect.

Most younger students are more influenced by the belonging needs and the esteem needs; therefore, these needs should be the targets to emphasize for goal setting by parents or other leaders. Parents ordinarily stress the physiological needs as goals for their children although these needs are not usually felt by students at an early age. As the child matures and begins to realize that he or she must begin planning to "face the world alone," those physiological needs begin to have a stronger meaning, and they become a target for goal setting by many students. Needs are analyzed in Chapter Four, and goals are analyzed in Chapter Eight.

Jealousy and Revenge

Yes, there really are people who demotivate themselves and avoid success by concentrating on jealousy or revenge against someone. In the workplace, peers are usually the objects of jealousy and leaders are usually the objects of revenge.

Jealousy is an emotional anchor that binds one into a fixed position. That fixed position will not allow one to focus on positive ways toward personal development. Jealousy obscures goals and leaves no place in one's rationality for positive motivation. Any motivation inspired by jealousy is negative motivation.

The desire for revenge is equally self-defeating. The self-demotivating effects from an "I'll get even with you" attitude is the major concern. Those who are influenced by this emotionalism ordinarily focus on another concern—that of trying to correct an injustice. While focusing on this right and justice campaign, one cannot progressively continue with a personal success plan. Frequently, perhaps usually, the act of revenge brings more problems and heartache to the initiator of those vengeful acts than to the target of those acts. Revenge usually backfires.

A special comment is not required here to associate jealousy and revenge that takes place within a work environment with that which occurs within a school environment. Jealousy and revenge are the same wherever they exist. They are high emotions that blind a person from real success goals and refocus that person toward negative energies. Those negative energies remove progressive motivations as a person's success guide. The removal of those progressive motivations creates a void filled with demotivation.

These internal demotivators are those conditions where a person, worker or student, demotivates himself or herself as a result of events or actions that he or she feels or perceives within himself or herself. These internal demotivators are self initiated and self created. Three external demotivators, also compared to conditions in a work environment, will be analyzed next to demonstrate the effect of outside influences.

Not Given Sufficient Responsibility

Most people, including employees, are more capable and anxious to do more than they are allowed to do. This creates a dilemma, particularly for employees and management. Management doesn't want to hire someone who can just barely do a job the same way, forever. If they were to hire this type of person, the burden on management would be a constant problem. Furthermore, management wouldn't have a valuable resource from which to promote, to fill vacancies or to facilitate expansion.

On the other hand, when management hires the best employees, those employees who can learn quickly and be expected to grow with the company, management doesn't usually have places for all those people to continue that growth. If management does a good job of hiring the most qualified employees, then all those employees will logically be expecting growth. The growth they are expecting is in the form of increasing opportunities, responsibility and authority.

If increasing growth opportunities aren't available for those employees, the most probable result is that they will become frustrated and demotivated. The answer to this dilemma is not simple. The point of view of management, naturally, will be different from that of the employee.

From the employee's perspective, there are some possible alternatives such as increasing his or her management qualifications or searching for opportunities at other companies. A different problem would be created from management's point of view. To develop those employees to the height of their potential would result in a continuing process of employee turnover and employee training if growth positions were not available within the company, since those employees would leave to accept higher jobs elsewhere. This normal workplace dilemma, lack of responsibility, causes many good employees to become demotivated.

How does this situation compare to that of students? Children have needs, feeling, desires and longings similar to those of adults. The mere fact that they are younger or smaller shouldn't suggest that their minds and thoughts have less capacity. A child might have less experience, but a child still has the basic capacity to rationalize events and to feel emotions and needs which are the same emotions and needs that adults feel. Many adults are really less competent to be contributing members of society than are many children, even with decades of "valuable" experience. A child is only a smaller and younger copy of an adult.

As discussed in Chapter Four, a child normally is not influenced by the basic physiological and survival needs. Those are fulfilled by simply being a member of a family that's expected to provide those essentials of food, water, shelter and clothing. A family, including the extended family, also is a source to fulfill many of the belonging needs. With these lower level needs basically fulfilled, this leaves the esteem needs as the critical motivator.

A child, as an adult, must have an opportunity to be responsible, or to feel responsible, for something meaningful as a source to fulfill that strong need. The reluctance of parents to allow children the level of responsibility of which they feel they are capable limits children's abilities to achieve that normal condition. This absence of a reasonable level of responsibility limits a child's opportunity to develop esteem—and as a result—becomes a demotivator.

The following list of duties, usually assigned to a child to increase responsibility, are not motivational or even sources of increased responsibility. They are simply chores that parents, themselves, don't enjoy doing. These chores certainly wouldn't be considered motivational for most adults. These include:

- Taking out the garbage
- Mowing the lawn
- Cleaning one's room
- Washing dishes
- Washing and polishing the family car

The following tasks, on the other hand, might allow a child to feel a level of responsibility that may transition into personal esteem:

- Allowing a child to pay the garbage bill
- Allowing a child to help design a flower bed
- Allowing a child to plan a family dinner
- Allowing a child to check the oil level in a car
- Allowing a child to help with any adult task

Although these tasks might seem simple and minor from an adult's perspective, they are important to a younger child for they represent a higher level of achievement and responsibility. They represent "meaningful work" and an acknowledgement of that child's importance. Absence of these meaningful opportunities tends to create demotivation rather than motivation for a child.

A Bad Environment

A bad work environment may or may not be a demotivator. It depends upon what's usually expected for that type of job and the homogeneous placement of the person actually doing the job. For example, a person who works outside most of the time in the sun, rain, cold and wind would consider that a bad work environment if that person didn't enjoy those conditions. He or she would probably become demotivated. A person who dislikes office work would probably prefer those outdoor conditions, consequently, that person probably wouldn't be demotivated by those conditions.

The other type of bad work environment, the mental one, is a source of demotivation for everyone associated with it. No matter what a person does in this situation that person cannot get adequately comfortable to allow concentration to give the best and most efficient efforts. It doesn't matter who or what causes a bad environment. The fact that the condition exists is the problem. Unless action is taken to correct a bad work environment, usually by the manager or the supervisor, demotivation will be generated by that environment. All members of a work group are equally responsible for creating a good working atmosphere. Everybody should do their share to improve the working environment.

A home environment and a school environment for a child should be compared with a work environment for a worker. A bad home or school environment for a child is as demotivational for a child as a bad work environment is for a worker. Parents who often accuse their children of not being motivated often are the cause of that lack of motivation. Schools that rate students as not sufficiently motivated to learn might be a major source of that lack of motivation.

For example, a home that doesn't provide basic family expectations of children will not encourage those children to remain highly motivated. These reasonable and basic expectations of family life include:

- The home is a place of comfortable refuge
- Parents show sincere affection for each other
- Parents demonstrate high ideals and aspirations
- Parents show that the child is loved, regardless of imperfections
- The child's privacy and needs are respected

Similar basic expectations exist in the school environment. Some of these basic expectations include:

- Each teacher will be fair, just and impartial

- A child's problem will not be regarded as simply an uneducated or irrational complaint
- A teacher will respect each child, and not embarrass any child in the classroom
- Each child should be protected from peer harassment
- The school environment should be free from harmful distractions

These expectations of home environments and school environments are normal conditions that a child needs to feel secure and comfortable. Herzberg (Chap. Four) identifies similar basics in the work environment as hygiene that's necessary to permit the development of motivation. A child without a basic level of comfort, or hygiene, cannot focus on more meaningful goals without those negative distractions.

Lack of Appreciation or Respect

This is a major source of demotivation for many employees. They feel that supervisors and managers don't show enough appreciation for what they do, and that they don't show enough respect for them personally, for who they are.

This feeling by employees may have an element of truth, or it may be based upon impressions and perceived innuendos. There are many managers and supervisors who sincerely appreciate employees' efforts and diligence, and who respect them as equal persons. They may be preoccupied with other things, however, and may not think of expressing their thoughts. There's also the possibility that some managers and supervisors don't know how to express their sincere feelings to employees. Many leaders have some of the same weaknesses as other people, and are limited in their abilities. This applies especially toward human relations and communications efforts.

On the other hand, there are self-centered managers and supervisors who think it's unnecessary to show appreciation or respect for their subordinates. They believe that workers are hired to be at work on time, and to produce while they are there. That's what they were hired for, and that's what they get paid for. While this belief is technically valid, it's counter to motivation efforts to improve productivity—which is the fundamental purpose for workers. Apprehension, fear and frustration are common in this work environment.

There's also the problem of some employees who cannot get enough love and attention to make them feel comfortable and appreciated. Even in a comfortable environment of mutual respect, these employees need constant reassurance that they are doing okay. Without this constant reassurance, they may become apprehensive and demotivate themselves by worrying about their level of appreciation.

Whether the feeling of lack of respect and appreciation is caused by fact, or by perceptions, it exists and it restricts motivation. The cause of this demotivation can be anywhere—employees, management, or in perceptions.

Children, students, have the same need for a feeling of respect and appreciation. Adults often forget these sensitivities of children, because they are only children. Some adults simply ignore this need, and others feel that they don't have enough time to waste with children. They are too busy trying to provide what those children really need: shelter, food and clothing. Many adults suggest that giving too much attention to a child "spoils" the child.

A child, as a normal person, must receive enough attention to make the child feel important. Most children function from feelings, not from historical references of achievement.Children are too young to have a long personal history, a list of achievements, significant material possessions or other reference points that signify high worldliness and status. They possess only themselves to suggest who they are.

Since the foundation that represents their existence is so small and narrowly defined, it must be nurtured. It must be specifically nurtured by the parent. If a parent must choose between spoiling a child by too much attention and making the child be more independent, the parent must spoil the child. A spoiled child will have more confidence and motivation to adjust to reality. A demotivated and emotionally scarred child might never fully recover.

These three examples demonstrate that students, as well as workers, face situations that tend to create conditions more suitable for demotivation than motivation. It's possible that these demotivation forces might be far stronger and more influential than the effects of any planned motivation efforts.

Historically, most emphasis to encourage people—especially workers and students—to be successful has been oriented toward finding ways to apply direct motivation principles. Demotivation has been recognized, somewhat, but it's never been given equal emphasis or equal status in the success planning process, usually identified as motivation.

Demotivation inherently contains a different application than does motivation. Motivation is based on theories and inferred influences and reactions; whereas, these examples identified in this chapter as demotivators really exist. They are not theoretical or imaginary. Real people feel the real effects of these conditions everyday. The impact of these demotivators is determined by one's susceptibility to these demotivators; and also by one's determination to reach a clearly identified goal.

Demotivators exist within one's own thought process, and in reality within one's everyday environment. Regardless of the existence of these demotivators, a person still has the choice and the personal power to decide if he or she will be negatively influenced by these demotivators, or if he or she really plans to be successful.

Summary

These three chapters in Part Three identify direct responsibilities of students and parents to help make the education system that exists more responsive. Some of these responsibilities also apply to teachers, for a supportive environment for efficient learning must be nurtured in every environment in which a student participates. Most of a student's time is occupied in a classroom and at home.

Chapter Eight emphasized that a student must plan to succeed to actually succeed. Without a success plan a student, as well as anyone else, has a failure plan. Even with a good success plan, however, many student fail because they aren't aware of natural obstacles to success. Those natural obstacles were identified in Chapter Nine to help students and their parents recognize them as normal obstacles when they occur. Chapter Ten identified a major source of failure as demotivation. Demotivation may cause failure even when a student has a strong desire to succeed.

The main goal of Part Three is to emphasize that the quality of a student's education and success is determined primarily by his or her home and cultural environment. A student must have a supportive family that understands the education process, and that provides an environment free of obstacles and demotivators. When those obstacles and demotivators exist, the parent must be there to nurture the student to prevent those obstacles and demotivators from creating demotivation.

Society is important in the education process. The education system itself is also important in the education process. Nothing, however, is as important to the effective education of a student as the student and his or her family. Society and the education system, in most cases, cannot adequately compensate for dysfunctional families or dysfunctional cultures.

CONCLUSION

One of the most amazing things about our education system is that it's designed backwards—or in reverse. Politicians, sociologists, bureaucrats, educators and even parents complain about the ineffectiveness of the school system, through high school level, yet no one really takes any fundamental action to improve the system. Enormous amounts of money are wasted on patching and fixing the education system—but there's never been a fundamental and revolutionary change to develop efficiency and effectiveness. The system is designed backwards for society has planned the education system before defining the purpose for education. This backward design creates serious problems.

Many schools have become battle zones where the interests of teachers, the interests of parents and the interests of society have higher priorities than the purpose of education or the interests of students. No one involved with the education process is blameless —including students.

Members of the Battle Zone

Teachers usually want more money and better conditions as compensation for working in that battle zone. Many teachers claim that the quality of education will improve if they receive higher salaries. Some teachers even walk picket lines under the guise of "better education." If teachers are really sincere they should stay in the classroom and prove that they deserve more pay. In a free market business economy that's the way higher pay is traditionally earned. Pay that's earned through demand and intimidation never satisfies that demand. It continues to rekindle itself.

In a free society higher qualified people choose a different career if he or she is dissatisfied with working conditions or pay in the current career. If Herzberg's motivation theory is considered valid more pay is not a motivator, it's a hygiene factor. Consequently, that would suggest that increased pay would not motivate teachers to teach better. A sincere teacher will teach at higher effectiveness for more personal reasons.

Many parents are frustrated for they expect their children simply to go to school and get a good education. Many of those parents who complain most about the failing quality from the education system haven't realized that, ordinarily, when their children fail to receive a quality education it's the parent's fault. Many homes are sources of despair, heartache and embarrassment for children instead of places for nurturing comfort. Often, a child succeeds in spite of the home environment rather than from guidance and support that it provides.

The parent of a student must learn to be that student's education partner, regardless of the education level or the teaching qualifications of the parent. The parent doesn't necessarily need to know course material. Simply applying the concepts detailed in Part Three will give sufficient comfort and support to a child.

Society remains confused regarding education, for society doesn't know the purpose for an education. Until a consensus for that purpose is determined it might be prudent if social and political leaders refrained from irrational political and social rhetoric. It's possible that the more they emphasize the inferiority of our education system the more damage they do to our education system. This recommendation is not likely to be followed for social and political reformers—candidates—would lose a campaign topic.

Students are the most oppressed, for they are the real frontline soldiers in this confused battle zone. No one is winning, for the enemy and battle lines are unknown. This condition is as if society were battling against nature's wind.

Recent Trends

The most recent education emphasis focuses on improving students' test scores by upgrading the skill levels and credentials of teachers. This emphasis is on teachers' performance and students' grades. This emphasis, once again, is a political decision. Any minor improvement in grade performance is normally politically exploited as a great victory in the educational war, when in fact, the situation might be nothing more than the rising curve of an up and down, long-term trend. In either case, the emphasis is targeted at grade results, with teacher accountability.

That emphasis is targeted at the wrong end of the education process for sustained learning by students. The emphasis must be targeted toward teaching students how to learn, not on teaching teachers how to teach. Students must be taught the success process —and it must include the parents' involvement in that learning process.

Increasing teachers' credentials and qualifications will most likely result only in increased teacher credentials and qualifications with an appropriate increase in salaries. Simply increasing teacher skills will not produce a more motivated or teachable student.

Student Options and Responsibilities

Many ideas and concepts have been analyzed in this small book regarding factors that affect a student's potential to become successful. These concepts have been explored to introduce the possibility that perhaps the education system that's intended to assist students to become successful is, in fact, one of the major obstacles to a student's success. The system, as it exists, restricts students without allowing reasonable alternatives. It also robs many of them of the esteem they must have to develop critical aspirations that are essential for goal setting, the foundation of success.

Students are encouraged to learn the success process so they may reach success, by themselves, regardless of obstacles.

They must actively absorb those parts of the education process that are positive and that contribute toward their success goals. They must also learn to reject, psychologically and emotionally, the negative stigma that results from the negative parts of the education process that they cannot influence or control.

A student may be successful in life regardless of an assigned or earned grade, or regardless of his or her intelligence level—within a normal range. The critical factors that determine success are:

- Sincerity
- Effort
- Determination
- Assignment of clear goals
- Support by one's family
- Focus on the objective

The most important success factor is simply to take the first active step to do something. These critical success factors are easily achievable by any student.

The Urgency

Although the emphasis and target of information in this book are oriented directly toward improving the quality of education and success of students, that purpose is not necessarily designed as the overriding urgency. A far more important purpose exists than merely to have better educated students. That important purpose is to increase the capability of each person in our country to make a positive contribution to the overall success of our country.

Actions, events, contributions and participation in any process are usually either positive or negative. Rarely will anything be neutral or inconsequential. Therefore, a person who's not prepared to make a positive contribution to the success of our country will most likely make a negative contribution. This means that if a person is not successful, at least to a certain level, that person becomes a drain on the productivity and the assets of our country.

Opportunity and productivity are the major and basic concepts that create the strength, viability and sustainability of a country. Without these things a country will have difficulty in continuing to exist.

To maintain that necessary level of productivity to insure that opportunities continue to exist and grow, we cannot allow ourselves and our country to be less than we can be. Good educations not only have intrinsic value that helps to create more enlightened people, good educations also allow us to maintain our productivity capacity to protect our country—The United States of America.

Can we afford to imagine the consequences of a world without a strong United States of America? If we allow our education system to degenerate, we or our children might have to face the realities of this question sometime in the future. This possibility is unnecessary, for all that's necessary to improve the effectiveness of the education system is simply to decide to do something—and then just do it.

I remain an optimist regarding the quality of America's youth. I feel certain that they will continue to be successful and will continue to make America the great hope for the world, despite our grandiose and confused attempts to guide them.

BIBLIOGRAPHY

1. Donald M. Levine and Mary Jo Bane,
The Inequality Controversy: Schooling and Distributive Justice
(Basic Books, Inc., Publishers, New York, 1975)

2. Ivor Morrish, *Disciplines of Education*
(George Allen & Unwin Ltd., Great Britain, 1967)

3. C. Northgate Parkinson, *Parkinson's Law*
(Houghton Mifflin Co., Boston, MA, 1957)

4. Abraham H. Maslow, *Motivation and Personality*
(Harper and Rowe, New York, NY, 1954)

5. Harry Maddox, *How To Study*
(Fawcett Publications, Inc., Greenwich, CT, 1963)

6. Frederick Herzberg, et. el., *The Motivation to Work*
(Wiley and Sons, New York, NY, 1959)

7. J. Jay Braun, Darwyn E. Linder, Isaac Asimov,
Psychology Today
(Random House, New York, NY, 1979) p. 411

8. Dale Carnegie, *How to Win Friends and Influence People*
(Simon and Schuster, Inc., New York, NY, 1977) p. 31

9. Bernard Berelson and Gary A. Steiner, *Human Behavior*
(Harcourt-Brace and World, Inc., 1967) Chap. 8

10. Norman Vincent Peale, *The Power of Positive Thinking*
(Prentice-Hall, New York, NY, 1952)

11. Albert J. Pautler, et. el., *Career Education*
(MSS Information Corporation, 1973)

12. Bertrand Russell, *Authority and the Individual*
(Beacon Press, Boston, 1949)

13. Robert H. Schuller, *Move Ahead With Possibility Thinking*
    (Fleming H. Revell Co., Old Tappan, NJ, 1978)

14. Joseph McKendrick, *Executive Excellence*
(Administrative Management Society, Willow Grove, PA, 1984)

15. Robert Zorn, *Speed Reading*
(Barnes & Noble Books, New York, NY, 1980)

16. Samuel Smith, *Read it Right and Remember What You Read*
(Barnes & Noble, New York, NY, 1970)

17. James D. Weinland, *How to Improve Your Memory*
(Barnes & Noble, New York, NY, 1968)

18. J.N. Hook, *Testmanship*
(Barnes & Noble, New York, NY, 1967)

19. Clifford T. Morgan, *Introduction to Psychology*
(McGraw-Hill Book Co., Inc., 1956)

20. Douglas McGregor, *The Human Side of Enterprise*
(McGraw Hill Book Co., Inc. New York, NY, 1960)

ADDITIONAL BIBLIOGRAPHY

Thomas A. Harris, *I'M OK—You're OK*
(Avon Books, New York, NY, 1969)

Denis Waitley, *The Psychology of Winning*
(Berkley Books, New York, 1979)

Gilbert Ryle, *The Concept of Mind*
(Barnes & Noble Books, New York, 1949)

Arthur L. Logan, *Remembering Made Easy*
(ARC Books, Inc., New York, NY, 1965)

Barbara B. Brown, *Stress and the Art of Biofeedback*
(Bantam Books, Inc., New York, 1978)

Wilfred Funk & Norman Lewis,
30 Days To A More Powerful Vocabulary
(Pocket Books, New York, NY, 1977)

Norman Vincent Peale, *You Can If You Think You Can*
(Fawcett Publications, Greenwich CT, 1974)

Edward De Bono, *The Five-Day Course In Thinking*
(A Signet Book by The New American Library,
New York, NY, 1968)

Philip G. Zimbardo, *Shyness*
(Jove Publications, Inc., New York, NY, 1978)

Michael B. Katz, *In The Shadow of the Poorhouse*
(Basic Books, Inc., Publishers, New York, 1986)

Ken Auletta, *The Underclass* (Vintage Books, New York, 1982)

Thomas J. Peters and Robert H. Waterman, Jr.,
In Search of Excellence
(Warner Books, New York, 1982)

Paul M. Stokes, *Total Job Training*
(American Management Association, 1966)

INDEX

A

Active Communications
72, 73
Admonish   49
Admonition   6
Adolescent years   140
Adults   2, 59, 66, 136,
142, 143, 146
Advice   6
Affection   48, 51
Aggression   132
Alcohol   128
Alienation   16, 17, 49, 63, 94
Ambivalence   4, 8, 10,
26, 27, 28, 29, 31,
32, 34, 35, 120, 124, 125
Anti-social behavior
92, 96, 97, 101, 128
Applicant   130, 139
Apprenticeships   17
Aspartame   128
Authority figures   45, 75,
123, 132, 137, 138
Avoiding demotivation
74, 107

B

Backfires   141
Barrier
cost   10, 75, 85, 88, 91, 100
doubt   23, 25, 26, 70, 84
freedom   17, 23, 29,
54, 66, 84
too busy   84, 146
Basics   7, 23, 25, 107,
110, 117, 145
Battle zone   149, 150
Behavior
operant   55, 56
respondent   55
Berelson and Steiner   73, 92

Black children   9
Books   49, 80, 81, 85, 87, 112
Bookstores   87
Brain cells   128
Business   16, 17, 18, 19,
23, 30, 32, 33, 34, 63,
73, 107, 125, 149
Business cycles   16

C

Campus Training   98
Cancer   101
Candidate   18, 37
Car   27, 140, 143
Career   6, 7, 8, 15, 17, 19,
20, 27, 29, 30, 31, 62,
64, 65, 66, 84, 86, 88,
89, 93, 99, 123, 139, 149
Carnegie, Dale   65
Children, minority   4
Choices, voluntary   56
Cognitive abilities   4
Comfort   54, 57, 122, 131,
140, 145, 150
Communications   48, 63, 69,
70, 71, 72, 73, 74, 83, 86,
87, 89, 108, 124, 125, 145
Comparing oneself   137, 138
Compensation   132, 133, 149
Comprehension   69, 70, 71,
73, 74, 111, 112
Consensus   4, 63, 150
Continuum   62, 64
Craftsmanship   17
Credentials   150
Criticism   23, 26, 32, 72, 125
Cubberly, Ellwood   30
Cultural background   5, 39,
42, 92
Cultural deprivation   119,
120, 122

ABOUT THE AUTHOR

Will Clark is an author and lecturer on leadership, work practices, motivation and study skills. He is the author of three books which include: *The Leadership Handbook—101 Ways To Be A Super Leader And Avoid Self-Destruction; Simply Success—The Employee's Handbook; and, Mississippi Yearning—For Success*. He also edits a statewide Chamber of Commerce newsletter.

As a retired Air Force officer, his experience in leadership and motivation began through military assignments in many cultural environments. He managed a Japanese workforce for two years, a Vietnamese workforce for one year and a Turkish workforce for two years. He was also a management and operational readiness inspector, evaluator and trainer for six years in Tactical Air Command of the U.S. Air Force. In this position he annually evaluated fifty military organizations to insure that logistical functions were efficiently managed to meet military requirements, such as a "Desert Storm" exercise. While he was assigned in Turkey, he also taught business courses from the City Colleges of Chicago to other American military people assigned there. He has a degree in business and management from the University of Nebraska and he completed Air Force Officer Candidate School and Air Command and Staff College.

He is the founder of Motivation Basics, a firm that provides leadership, workplace and student motivational training. He also provides motivational training to civic and charitable organizations.

'GET MORE FUN BOOKS FROM R & E AND SAVE!

TITLES	ORDER #	PRICE
Person-To-Person *Awareness Techniques for Counselors and Parent Educators*	738-2	$15.95
Towards a Thinking Curriculum *Making Right Behavior Part of our Society*	854-0	10.95
How the Universe Was Born *The Big-Bang Concept Buried!*	858-3	11.95
For Teachers Only: *Personal and Confidential*	889-3	9.95
Play on Words: Klever Word Puzzles for Very Klever People *A Fast Laugh—With Quick Wit Word Puzzles*	969-5	9.95
Revenge in the Classroom: Skool Kartoons for Everyone *You'll Love to Laugh and Share the Humor of Education!*	966-0	$9.95
The Presentation Handbook: *How To Prepare Dynamic and Non-Technical Presentations* *What Makes a Good Instructor and How To Become One*	872-9	14.95
Statistics In Science *A Student's and Teacher's Manual For Science,* *Math & Computer Science Projects & Experiments*	905-9	14.95

ORDER ANY 4 TITLES & GET ONE FREE—PLUS FREE POSTAGE!

Please rush me the following books. I want to save by ordering four books and receive a free book plus free postage. Orders under four books please include $3.00 shipping. CA residents add 8.25% tax.

PAYMENT METHOD
- ❏ Enclosed Check or Money Order
- ❏ Master Card
- ❏ Visa

YOUR ORDER

ORDER #	QUANTITY	UNIT PRICE	TOTAL PRICE

Card Expires _____

Signature _____

RUSH SHIPMENT TO:

(Please print)

Name _____

Organization _____

Address _____

City/State/Zip _____

R & E Publishers ● P.O. Box 2008 ● Saratoga, CA 95070
● (408) 866-6303 ● FAX (408) 866-0825